101 Grow to Eat Ideas

10 9 8 7 6

Published in 2007 by BBC Books,
an imprint of Ebury Publishing
A Random House Group Company

Book Design © Woodlands Books Limited 2007
All photographs and text © BBC Magazines 2007
All the ideas contained within this book first appeared in BBC
Gardeners' World Magazine

All rights reserved. No part of this publication may be reproduced,
stored in a retrieval system, or transmitted in any form or by any
means, electronic, mechanical, photocopying, recording or otherwise,
without the prior permission of the copyright owner

The Random House Group Limited Reg. No. 954009

Addresses for companies within the Random House Group can be
found at www.randomhouse.co.uk

A CIP catalogue record for this book is available from the British Library

The Random House Group Limited supports The Forest Stewardship
Council (FSC), the leading international forest certification organization.
All our titles that are printed on Greenpeace approved FSC certified
paper carry the FSC logo. Our paper procurement policy can be found
at www.rbooks.co.uk/environment

To buy books by your favourite authors and register for offers visit
www.rbooks.co.uk

Printed and bound by Firmengruppe APPL, aprinta druck,
Wemding, Germany
Colour origination by Dot Gradations Ltd

ISBN: 978 0 563 53927 8

Gardeners'
World magazine

101 Grow to Eat Ideas

RECIPES THAT TASTE AS GOOD AS THEY LOOK

Editor
Ceri Thomas

BOOKS

Contents

Introduction

There are few things as satisfying as eating delicious fruit and veg you've grown yourself. You'll never have tasted anything as fresh and full of flavour, and you'll find it impossible to go back to 'cotton wool' tomatoes and limp lettuce.

This improved taste is all down to how little time home-grown produce spends journeying between the ground and your plate; there's no chance of it losing its juicy freshness or for its sugars to be converted into dull-tasting starch. How can something that's flown half-way across the world to get to a supermarket compare with veg that has only travelled ten yards to your cooking pot?

Growing your own produce also allows you to control its cultivation. If you don't want to eat chemical residues, then this is your opportunity to avoid them. You can also experiment with delicious and unusual varieties that would never be found in a supermarket.

We at *Gardeners' World Magazine* have picked 101 of our favourite tips to help you get more from growing fruit and veg, whether you've been doing it for years or whether it's the first time you've tried. And you don't need a large garden or allotment to put these ideas into practise, because there are also suggestions for getting great crops in containers.

So, read on and you'll never eat a bland-tasting fruit or veg again.

Ceri Thomas
Gardeners' World Magazine

Grow spuds in a pot

Time to plant: March/April

If you don't have much open ground in your garden you can still grow potatoes; simply put them in a container and enjoy fresh young spuds that little bit earlier.

Grow your potatoes in a container measuring a minimum of 30cm (1ft) deep and wide, but if it is a bit bigger, so much the better. A 45cm (18in) pot will hold three tubers of a single variety.

Fill the pot to halfway with multi-purpose compost, or an equal parts mix of this and a John Innes loam-based compost. Good drainage is essential, so put a few pieces of broken pot at the bottom of the container first. Gently nestle each tuber into the compost with the shoots (known as eyes) uppermost, and cover them with a few inches of compost.

Keep the compost just moist and wait for those shoots to appear. As the shoots form, earth up around them by adding more compost. The potates will be ready to harvest once the flowers start to open.

TIP
Fast-growing early potato varieties are among the most rewarding to grow. Planted in March, you'll enjoy delicious new potatoes in June and July.

Autumn fire   Time to plant: late May

This fruitful gathering has great autumnal appeal, coming into its own in the latter half of the summer when many other containers are looking tired.

The centrepiece of this container, the chilli 'Apache' grows to only 45cm (18in) high but produces lots of small, medium-hot chillies that are highly ornamental and really spice up a meal. A colourful alternative is 'Fiesta', with fruits that vary from yellow and purple to orange-red.

The copper-brown grass, *Carex comans* here creates a feathery backdrop, while the contrasting steel-blue leaves of *Koeleria glauca* and bronze uncinia fill out the front of the container. Any combination of dwarf grasses would work equally well – try yellow-leaved *Acorus gramineus* 'Hakuro-nishiki' and blue fescue.

Position a *Lotus* studded with orange-red blooms – to echo the chilli fruits – at the edge of the pot where its sea-green, needle-like leaves can cascade freely.

Plant up in late May when the danger of frost has passed, or any time during the summer. Plant the tallest grass at the back and the chilli in the centre, allowing it plenty of room to develop.

Place the container in a warm, sheltered spot to encourage the chillies to ripen.

TIP
Start feeding chillies with a high-potash liquid feed as soon as the first flowers appear.

Tomato basket

Time to plant: May

Tumbling tomatoes produce a mass of stems that drip with cherry-sized fruits. Given the chance, a single plant will fill a hanging basket on its own, but here it is accompanied by curly leaved parsley and trailing black-eyed Susan (*Thunbergia alata*).

Yellow, orange and cream-coloured blooms of thunbergia will set off brightly coloured tomatoes to perfection. Its twining stems will also hide the basket chains and trail over the sides as it scrambles haphazardly through the tomato plant.

Parsley, the perfect herb for garnishing salads and all manner of other dishes, contributes a pool of fresh green leaves that should be picked young for the best flavour.

Pick the tomatoes as they ripen to encourage the plant to produce more fruit. Over the summer, gently train the shoots of the thunbergia in the direction you wish them to grow and trim away any leaves that shade the ripening tomatoes.

Fully laden with fruit, the tomato plant will be quite heavy, so make sure the basket is hung from a strong bracket.

Water daily, or twice a day if the weather is very hot or windy, and feed with tomato food once a week.

TIP
Tomatoes and parsley are thirsty plants, so add a few water-retaining crystals to the compost when planting to reduce your watering chores.

Lavender and thyme basket

Time to plant: April/May

The beautiful herbs in this hanging basket will delight the eye all summer and are a treat both for the taste buds and nose.

Choose a dwarf lavender such as the compact-growing 'Bella Series', which is available in a range of colours including white, pink and mauve-blue. Use several different varieties of thyme for a good mix of colour and flavour.

Lavender and thyme are both drought-tolerant, however, you will need to water the basket regularly, so add water-retaining crystals to the compost when planting and mix in slow-release fertilizer to keep them nourished. Remove faded blooms to encourage more flowers.

Position the basket in a sheltered spot, preferably where you can take a reviving sniff every time you pass by. At the end of the summer, plant out the thymes and lavender into a sunny, well-drained spot where they can give you years of pleasure.

TIP
The chopped leaves and flowers of lavender can be added to biscuit mixtures to give them a distinctive taste and aroma, while thymes are excellent for bringing flavour to both meat and fish dishes, or in stuffing mixes.

Herb pyramid

Time to plant: April/May

Herbs are the perfect plant for growing by the back door, then within seconds of harvesting they are in the kitchen, ensuring their freshest flavours.

To make the pot pyramid, start off with a wide container and fill it halfway with John Innes No 3 compost. Adding extra grit to the compost gives the herbs the good drainage they enjoy.

Choose a second pot that, when placed inside the first one, will leave a band around the rim large enough to plant in. Fill in around the second pot with more compost, then repeat the process with a smaller, third pot.

Once you have your pyramid of pots, plant it up with your favourite herbs and put it in a sunny spot. Turn the pot regularly to give all the plants equal sunlight. Keep it well watered and it should provide regular harvests of fresh herbs all summer long.

TIP
A pyramid pot creates a simple feature for a sunny site, but do plant it up in situ, as the completed display will be very heavy to move.

Super scents
Time to plant: March/May

Get the most from this container and put it near a path or on your patio. Every time you brush past, this highly aromatic collection of herbs will release their delicious perfumes.

Most herbs originate in hot, dry climates and dislike British cold, wet winters. So growing such herbs in pots is the perfect solution, as they can easily be brought indoors for the winter.

Serrated-leaved *Lavandula* x *christiana* makes an attractive alternative to ordinary lavender. It's on the tender side, but if you bring it indoors when the weather turns cold it will get it through the winter unscathed. Woolly thyme (*Thymus pseudolanuginosus*) also benefits from winter protection as it hates wet ground. This thyme has wonderful tactile leaves, which are topped by pretty pinky-mauve flowers which cover the plant all summer.

Many herbs have colourful foliage, and sages offer some of the widest varieties. In this pot we've used golden-leaved sage (*Salvia officinalis* 'Icterina'), but you'll also find purple and tricolour types on offer. All sages produce purple-blue flowers in summer and are delicious in cooking.

A prostrate rosemary placed at the front of this pot helps soften its edges. There are a number of varieties which have this unusual habit, such as *Rosmarinus officinalis* Prostratus Group, and they make a useful alternative to the more commonly-seen upright sorts. They're just as tasty in cooking and are covered in flowers from spring onwards.

TIP
Herbs love sunshine, so put them in the sunniest spot you can. A south-facing spot is ideal as they can bake in the sun all day.

Magic carpet

Time to plant: March/May

Recycled containers add an individual touch to your displays. The only limit to what you can use is your imagination.

Indulge in a scented carpet of colourful leaves with this display of different types of thyme. Most garden centres will have a reasonable selection of varieties on offer, but to get the widest choice, buy your plants from a specialist herb nursery.

This display uses no less than six varieties of thyme: broad-leaved (*Thymus pulegioides*), lemon-scented (*T.* x *citriodorus*), golden (*T. pulegioides* 'Aureus'), variegated (*T. citriodorus* 'Golden Queen'), silvery (*T. vulgaris* 'Silver Posie'), and common thyme (*T. vulgaris*). All these herbs enjoy a sunny spot and well-drained compost – use a loam-based John Innes compost with extra grit added to improve the drainage.

As an evergreen herb, thyme can be picked for the kitchen at any time of year, and any leaves you can't use straightaway can be dried for use later on. They don't need much maintenance either. Just give the plants a quick trim if they start to become unruly.

TIP
Make sure your container drains freely by filling the base with gravel or broken up chunks from polystyrene trays before adding compost.

Purple magic
Time to plant: March/May

Make the most of herbs with colourful leaves to create a pot that looks as good as it tastes.

Dark green rosemary (*Rosmarinus officinalis* 'Blue Lagoon') takes centre stage in this dramatic container and gives height to the display. Its spiky leaves taste delicious with lamb and can also be used medicinally. 'Blue Lagoon' is a particularly pretty variety from early spring, when it is covered in deep blue flowers.

Silver-leaved curry plants (*Helichrysum italicum*) and purple-leaved sage (*Salvia officinalis* 'Purpurascens') alternate around the edge of the pot, interspersed with purple-flowered violas. Curry plants earn their name thanks to their amazingly pungent scent, although they're not actually used in curries. They make very ornamental plants, though, with their silvery leaves and yellow flowers.

Purple sage is another herb which is useful in cooking, and it tastes as good as the plain-green variety. The young leaves of this plant are dark purple, gradually fading to green as they age.

TIP
This handsome combination of favourite herbs will last all summer. However, once plants begin to outgrow their space, simply move them out into the garden and replace with young plants raised from cuttings.

A taste of the Orient

Time to plant: May/June

It's surprising how many oriental vegetables and herbs can be grown successfully in Britian. This group of containers features some of the most popular types.

Lemon grass forms a big, impressive plant once it gets going, and is the centrepiece of our group. Its stems have an intense lemon-like flavour that's delicious in Thai cookery. The plant can be harvested all summer long, then when autumn arrives it should be left to go dormant, then brought into a frost-free place over winter.

Thai basil has a different flavour to the Italian types of this popular herb. It's a favourite ingredient in Thai and Vietnamese cooking. Plants are easy to raise from seed each spring.

The final two pots contain pak choi and mixed oriental salad leaves. You'll find a good selection of seeds available in mail-order seed catalogues. Their only peculiarity is that they shouldn't be sown until after midsummer in the UK. This is because they have a tendency to produce flowers instead of leaves if sown when the days are lengthening. Wait until midsummer – when the days start to shorten again – and you won't have any problems.

TIP

Planting in separate pots means you can get ahead on the lemon grass and Thai basil to get the most from them over the summer. Then you can add the pak choi and oriental salad leaves to the display at their optimum planting time.

Wacky wellies   Time to plant: April/May

Containers don't have to be boring; all sorts of objects can be used instead of conventional pots – including cheap and colourful wellies! We've finished off the display with a watering can filled with veg, but use whichever object takes your fancy!

To plant your wellies, start by drilling some drainage holes in the soles. These are vital as they allow excess water to escape. Then put some stones or pieces of polystyrene packaging inside to further improve drainage.

Support the legs of the wellies and stop them falling over by putting three canes inside each boot, cutting them so their tops are hidden when the compost is added.

Finally, fill the boots with multipurpose compost and then either sow or plant your chosen veg. For an extra flourish you could even cut off the toe of the boot and squeeze in a drought-tolerant thyme.

TIP
Wellies make surprisingly useful containers as their length gives space for roots to grow undisturbed. They are perfect for root veg such as carrots and parsnips, and long-rooted herbs such as chervil.

Salsa! Time to plant: April/May

If you're a fan of Mexican food, this colourful collection of pots is perfect for you. It contains everything you need to make your own delicious spicy salsa.

Chillies are best grown in pots so they can be easily moved indoors when the weather cools. Larger-fruited varieties are great to flavour stuffing as well as salsa. The keys to success with chillies are to feed once a week with tomato food as soon as the first fruits appear and to keep the compost moist – dry conditions will cause the flower buds to drop.

Tomatoes also do well in containers, as long as they're big enough. Large-fruited tomato varieties ripen best in the greenhouse, but smaller types do well outdoors. Keep an eye out for dwarf varieties such as 'Tumbler', which have been specially bred for growing in pots. Like the chillies, they also need regular feeding and watering.

Sowing a pinch of coriander seeds every few weeks during spring and summer will produce a regular supply of fresh leaves. If your plants do begin to flower, don't despair – not only are the white blooms very attractive, but you'll also get coriander seeds, which are equally useful in cooking.

TIP
There is an amazing number of varieties of chillies to choose from, but one good piece of advice is to check how hot the fruits promise to be – some can be absolutely scorching and you might find them inedible!

The three sisters

Time to plant: April/May

Named by the Native Americans, the 'three sisters' – pumpkins, sweetcorn and beans – were grown together as the plants naturally help one another. Sweetcorn provides a climbing stalk for the beans; beans provide nitrogen to nourish the sweetcorn, and pumpkins cover the soil and help suppress weeds.

Look out for dwarf varieties that are perfectly suited to growing in containers. 'Hestia' is an excellent dwarf runner bean that doesn't climb.

Alternatively, use dwarf French beans; you'll find colourful yellow and purple-podded varieties as well as the usual green ones. To keep their colour when cooking, microwave or steam them instead of boiling.

A delicious compact pumpkin perfect for growing in a pot is 'Baby Bear', which you harvest in autumn before first frosts.

As a final touch, add a few nasturtium plants; their colourful flowers will brighten up the area around the base of the sweetcorn, and when picked they will add a peppery flavour to salads.

TIP
Use a container large enough to accommodate three or four sweetcorn plants. As they are wind pollinated, planting them in close proximity should ensure good pollination, resulting in well-filled cobs.

Strawberries from seed

Time to sow: March–April

The traditional way to raise strawberries is to root runners, but if you don't have a stock of plants to propagate from, and the price of new strawberry plants puts you off growing them, why not raise your own from seed?

Great varieties of strawberries are available as seeds at a fraction of the cost of plants; and if you sow them in early spring, you should get fruits the same year.

Early sowing is essential for the best crop in the same year, but remember that strawberries are perennials so they will flower and fruit again for several years. Sow any time between March and the end of April in a heated propagator in your greenhouse or on a windowsill – setting the temperature at 18–21°C (65–70°F) for the best germination.

Strawberry seeds are very small, so take care when tipping them out into your hand. Dampen your finger to pick up a few seeds at a time and sow on the compost surface.

Pot up seedlings into 7.5cm (3in) pots, keep them in a greenhouse or cold frame and feed weekly as they develop. Once plants are looking sturdy with a good rootball, plant them outside in an open, sunny position. Growing strawberries in large pots seems to help deter slugs.

TIP
You'll find a range of different varieties on sale in mail-order catalogues and in the garden centre. Tiny alpine strawberries are particularly sweet.

Give melons a go

Time to plant: late spring

One of the most refreshing fruits to eat on a hot summer's day is a melon, with its sweet juicy flesh. Although the melons we buy from supermarkets are grown in warmer climes, it is possible to grow your own in a greenhouse.

Melons are closely related to cucumbers and require similar growing conditions to thrive.

The secret to producing good fruit is to not sow the seed until late spring when the days are warmer, and the plants will develop much faster.

Melons need warmth, water and food to grow well. They can be quite vigorous, so regular pruning is needed to keep them under control and ensure they put their energies into fruiting, not foliage.

Grow plants in containers 30cm (1ft) in diameter. Plant the melon in the centre on a low mound with the compost level graduating down. This helps to prevent water standing around the base of the stem, which can lead to rotting.

Help the fruiting process by hand pollinating the flowers. Strip the petals from the male flower and rub against the female flower (the one with slight swellings behind the flowerheads).

Provide plants with a support to grow up and water regularly and feed on a weekly basis. Thin out the tiny fruits to leave a maximum of four melons per plant.

TIP
Look out for small cracks appearing around the stalks of melons – this will tell you that your fruit is ready to harvest.

Protect fruit blossom

Time to do: spring

The sight of a fruit tree covered in blossom in spring is breathtaking, and this makes them worthy of a place in the garden.

Blossom is very susceptible to frost, so you must provide cover if it is forecast. If frost damages the blossom you will not only lose the flowers, but it can also have a disastrous effect on the crop.

Draping horticultural fleece over a fairly small tree works well, and if you want to keep it that bit more snug, use a double layer. You can even use old net curtains. Wherever you live, but especially if your garden is subjected to fierce winds, make sure that you anchor the fleece well.

Pollinating insects will still need to reach the blossom, so the fleece or other covering must be removed each morning, then replaced as necessary. It may be time consuming, but it's well worth the effort.

TIP
Whatever you use to protect blossom, make sure it is permeable and will allow moisture out and air in. A solid layer, such as polythene sheeting, causes a lot of problems with muggy, damp air and condensation.

Feed and weed
Time to do: spring

Your soil is still moist and just starting to warm up in spring, which makes it the perfect time to mulch around the base of fruit plants.

Remove any weeds and gently dig over the soil surface (if it is compacted) before applying mulch. A thick layer of mulch nourishes the plants and also reduces the amount of weeds reappearing in spring.

Lay a mulch of manure, compost or other suitable material in a circle about 45cm (18in) in diameter – or even wider if you have the space. Provided the soil is moist when mulched, this blanket will help reduce moisture loss from the soil and will also insulate beneath the soil surface.

It is important not to smother the plants when adding a layer of mulch, and it must not touch the stems or trunks as this could encourage diseases, stem rotting and generally make the plants struggle.

When you've finished mulching, not only will the plants benefit but your beds will look neat, tidy and well cared for.

TIP
Raspberries in particular really benefit from a good mulch. Their roots are especially vulnerable to drought as they sit near the surface of the soil, where the ground is driest.

Success with strawberries

Time to do: spring–summer

A few weeks of warm weather in late spring, combined with some of that omnipresent rain, is enough to get strawberry plants moving at an incredible rate.

With a plentiful supply of healthy, bright green foliage, fresh flowers will open daily and more and more fruits will form. Inspect both the flowers and the fruits regularly, and if any are showing signs of problems, pinch them off.

Frost is the main danger for strawberry flowers. If you spot a damaged fruit, remove it promptly so the plant does not lose energy and so that the remaining fruits can benefit.

Once the strawberries start to form in earnest, place a thick layer of dry straw beneath each truss of fruits. This holds them clear of the ground, reducing slug and snail damage, and it also helps to keep the fruits clean. On heavy-cropping varieties, so many trusses form that it's best to simply put straw down over the entire area to start with. You can buy special strawberry mats, but they are often too small and tend to buckle, which means they don't retain moisture in the way a thick straw mulch does.

TIP
If you live in a frost-prone area, protect your plants by covering them with cloches or horticultural fleece.

Make room for raspberries

Time to plant: spring or autumn

Choose a couple of varieties with different fruiting times and you can enjoy juicy raspberries from summer until first frosts.

Raspberry canes should be planted by early March. It pays to ensure that the soil has been well manured in advance. If the soil is heavy, then incorporating plenty of grit should improve drainage, or you could try planting the canes on a slight mound.

Summer-fruiting raspberries need a sturdy support system of tanalised posts with struts and galvanised training wires. It is easiest to get this in place before planting.

Autumn-fruiting raspberries form a denser thicket of canes than their summer cousins.

Always choose healthy-looking canes – preferably those certified as being virus-free – and plant them 38–45cm (15–18in) apart, with about 1.8m (6ft) between the rows. It is important to spread their roots well so that they will form a plentiful supply of new canes.

Once the canes are in position, cut them back to about 25cm (10in) above soil level.

TIP
'Glen Ample', 'Glen Moy' and 'Glen Prosen' are all great summer-fruiting varieties, while 'Autumn Bliss', 'Joan J' and 'Fallgold' will extend the harvest into autumn.

Preserve your fruit crop

So you've harvested your fruits and this year's bumper crop could feed an army, but if you pack it away and preserve it, you could be eating home-grown produce all winter.

Some fruits are perfect for storing in the freezer, especially raspberries. Lay them out individually on a tray, making sure they're not touching, and freeze them overnight. Once frozen you can put them in an airtight plastic box and they will stay separate; and unlike strawberries, they won't turn to mush once they've thawed. This method also works well for currants, blackberries and gooseberries.

Apples and pears are best stored immediately after harvesting – although don't bother with early varieties of apple as these don't keep well. Select only unblemished fruits, rejecting any with bruises, holes, or signs of disease or pest attack.

Ideally you should wrap each piece of fruit in a piece of greaseproof paper and place it in a wooden slatted box so that air can circulate around it. Or place apples in a plastic bag pierced with several holes.

Leave the fruit in a cool, dark place and it should keep for several months. Check it every so often and remove any fruits that show signs of going off.

TIP
Use up gluts of fruit by blending them into juices or smoothies. Drunk fresh, they're packed with healthy vitamins and anti-oxidants.

Root new strawberry plants

Time to do: late summer

Strawberries are one of the most delicious fruits of the summer garden. After a few years, though, plants tend to become less productive, but they can be easily and cheaply replaced.

Strawberry plants are ridiculously easy to grow. They thrive in a sunny spot and the only other real requirement is that the compost is kept moist at all times.

Once strawberries have finished fruiting, in late summer, clear away the straw from around the plants. Now you can easily get at the 'runners' – the small plants sent out on long shoots by the parent plant. Choose a runner with healthy green leaves and, leaving it attached to its parent, pin it onto the surface of a pot filled with multipurpose compost. A U-shaped staple, or a piece of wire, is perfect for holding it in place.

When the new plants are strongly rooted and living an independent life, they can be severed from the parent plant. Remove them from their pots and plant them in their new home in the ground, or plant into larger patio pots and baskets.

TIP
When planting strawberries, press the soil down around the roots. To test if they're planted firmly enough, gently tug one of the leaves; if the plant lifts from the ground, replant it more snugly.

Pick pears in their prime

Time to do: late summer–autumn

There's something wonderful about biting into a freshly picked pear that's so ripe it sends juice running down your chin. But how can you be sure that your pears are ready for picking?

When they are ready to pick, the fruit should still be quite firm, although not rock hard, and with most varieties the skin colour becomes a slightly paler shade of green.

If you are uncertain, carefully cup the fruit in your hand and gently, but firmly, give it a slight twist. If it is ripe, the fruit stalk should break from the spur and you'll be left holding a delicious pear.

For some early varieties the bite test is probably the most reliable way of seeing if the fruit is ready for eating. Pick the fruit and take a bite. If it is still hard and relatively flavourless, then wait a week or perhaps more before trying again.

When picked, bring them into a warm room to ripen, or store in a cool space for later use – but don't store in polythene bags, as this encourages rot.

TIP
Try stewing peeled whole pears and eating them with butterscotch sauce. Delicious!

Juicy gooseberries

Time to plant: autumn–spring

Gooseberries are one of the easiest fruits you can grow, producing heavy crops of green, yellow or red fruits even in their first year.

As soon as the crop is just about ready to pick, consider netting the bush in order to keep those succulent berries for your own use, rather than have the whole lot consumed by the local bullfinch population. Over smaller plants, hold the net in place with bamboo canes topped with inverted flowerpots to keep it in position. Always ensure the net is firmly anchored at the base, otherwise the birds may find a way in at ground level.

Drenching the soil around the bush with water on a regular basis will help produce larger fruits. Around 25–50 litres (5.5–11 gallons) per square metre (square yard) should keep the roots moist for a good while, especially if the soil is covered by a mulch.

Be regular with your watering and keep the moisture supply coming consistently at the roots once the fruits are ripening – erratic watering will cause your gooseberries to split.

Good varieties of gooseberries to look out for are 'Invicta' and 'Whinham's Industry'.

TIP
A moist soil will help to keep your gooseberries free from powdery mildew, which covers the berries in a white coating.

Jewels of summer

Time to plant: late autumn– early spring

Grow a selection of currants along with strawberries and raspberries and you can create the most delicious summer puddings and jams, or just enjoy handfuls of fruit fresh from the plant.

Redcurrants, whitecurrants and blackcurrants have to be among the prettiest fruits you can grow. Redcurrants in particular look like clusters of jewels as they weigh down the branches. They are easy to pick off the plant and can then be removed from those irritating twiggy bits using a fork.

Currants ripen fast, so unless you are quick off the mark, or have them properly netted or in a fruit cage, the birds will often get there first.

Red- and whitecurrants are easy to train in shapes like cordons and fans to make the most of a small space. Prune red- and whitecurrants in winter, and blackcurrants after fruiting.

TIP
Look out for the following varieties: redcurrants – 'Red Lake' and 'Jonkeer van Tets'; whitecurrants – 'Versailles Blanche' and 'White Grape'; blackcurrants – 'Ben Lomond' and 'Ben Sarek'.

Prune raspberry canes

Time to do: autumn and spring

Once the very last of the summer-fruiting raspberries have been eaten, it is time to set to and sort out the canes.

Cut down to ground level all canes that have borne a summer crop of fruits, which will allow plenty of space for the newer canes to produce their crop next year.

Choose seven or eight sturdy, healthy-looking canes per plant, then train them into the system of support wires. Space them well so that each has plenty of room – a distance of 7.5–10cm (3–4in) between them works well. Snip out the remaining canes with secateurs.

Tie the canes into position using garden twine. Invariably some of the canes are taller than the top wire, but rather than cutting these off, loop them over and tie them back into the top wire. They should be cut back to about 15cm (6in) above this wire in early to mid-February. It may sound crazy doing it this way, but if pruned back in late autumn the canes tend to fruit less well the next year, so that extra bit of twine tying is time well invested.

TIP
Autumn-fruiting raspberries, such as 'Autumn Bliss', are even easier to prune than summer-fruiting varieties; simply cut back the canes to ground level in February.

Plant bare-root fruit trees

Time to plant: late autumn–early spring

Bare-root plants are available from late autumn to early spring and offer a cheap way of buying fruit trees.

Take your fruit tree and spread the roots out well in a prepared planting hole. Scoop soil back into the hole, checking regularly that the stem is not being buried too deeply. This is because the graft point must be kept above ground level, otherwise the graft could fail or the tree could produce growth from the rootstock instead of the upper portion. (The graft point is a distinctive lump on the stem, just above the roots.)

Lay a straight bamboo cane or small plank across the top of the planting hole to make it easier to check that the planting depth is correct. If in doubt, add or remove soil as appropriate.

Add your tree stake now to minimise damage to the roots. Once the tree and stake are in place, firm the soil around them well with your boot (but not too hard if the soil is heavy), and check the level one last time.

Make sure the trees are kept well watered for the next few months.

TIP

If possible, plant your fruit trees as soon as you get them home or receive them through the post. The roots may need trimming first to remove any that are dead, damaged or excessively long.

Choose the right rootstock

Fruit trees are propagated onto rootstocks; and this is the most important factor in determining the vigour and eventual size of the tree.

When choosing your fruit tree, you will need to make sure you buy one on the right rootstock so that you get a tree that is most suitable for the size of your garden. The tree will have been joined ('grafted') onto a suitable rootstock, as varieties do not breed true from seed.

For plums, 'St Julien A' is a semi-vigorous rootstock suitable for most soil conditions, including relatively poor soil and grassed orchards. A mature tree will reach 3–3.6m (10–12ft) with a spread of 3.6m (12ft). If you want a smaller tree, try the dwarfing rootstock 'Pixy' which reaches 2.4–3m (8–10ft), but this is only worthwhile on good soil.

Most pear trees are grafted onto quince rootstock. 'Quince A' rootstock is the most popular. Trees grafted onto this will reach 3–6m (10–20ft) high. You'll also find pears on 'Quince C' rootstock, but these trees won't grow quite as large, as the growth slows once the tree starts to produce fruit. 'Quince C' trees will also fruit a fortnight earlier than other rootstocks.

TIP
If you want a dwarf apple tree in a small garden, then 'M9' is the recommended rootstock; 'M27' is smaller, but requires very fertile soil. For larger trees, try 'M26' or 'MM106'.

Fruitful small plots

Time to plant: late autumn/early spring

Even the smallest garden can squeeze in a fruit tree or two if they are trained in a fan shape, so that they lie flat against a fence or wall.

Fan-training a fruit tree not only means it takes up the least amount of space but also provides it with extra protection from the elements – helping more sensitive fruits, such as peaches and nectarines, produce successful crops. It is also easier to protect a fan-trained tree with netting or fleece than a free-standing one.

When and how to prune depends on the type of fruit, but for sweet cherries like the one in the picture, it's worth choosing two or three shoots on each branch and tying them in to fill any gaps in the framework. Pick shoots that will be easy to train in this way, then prune out the rest.

On more established fans, you will also need to tie in suitable shoots to fill gaps. Prune back the shoots that you don't need to about five or six leaves. Do this in summer, before you put netting over the tree to protect the fruit from birds.

Feed your tree in early spring with sulphate of potash to promote flowering and fruiting, then again as soon as the fruits begin to ripen.

TIP
You can have a go at fan-training your fruit trees, or you can save yourself the work and buy trees that have already been trained.

Get early rhubarb

Time to do: early to mid-winter

There is something immensely comforting about rhubarb, especially when it is buried beneath a thick layer of crumble and custard.

Rhubarb is a delicious treat that can be enjoyed as early as February or March by forcing crops. This involves keeping the plants in the dark, which encourages an earlier crop of tender sticks.

Forcing is easily done using traditional terracotta rhubarb forcers, or even a black plastic dustbin. The important thing is to get your forcer of choice in place over your rhubarb plant by mid-winter.

When the crop, whether forced or not, is ready, always pull the stalks rather than cutting them. You may feel that you are removing pieces of the plant in the process, but doing it this way hugely reduces the risk of the plants developing potentially fatal rots.

Save your sharp knife to cut off the foliage and the white end of each stick while you are in the garden and add them to the compost heap.

TIP
'Valentine' is a great variety as it has a delicious flavour and very tender stalks. Other varieties worth growing include 'Early Champagne' and 'Stockbridge Arrow'.

Spring clean your greenhouse

Time to do: early spring

After winter and before you start sowing the summer's seeds is the ideal time to give your greenhouse a good clean.

Light levels begin to increase in spring, but it is still essential to maximise all light. To ensure that seedlings and young plants inside the greenhouse get as much sunlight as possible, give the glass a good spring clean, inside and out. Start on the inside – you'll be amazed at how much gunk you can clear. An old washing-up brush and some soapy water, combined with a good deal of elbow grease, works wonders.

Glazed edges and the frame also need a clean up, as they are particularly good at harbouring dirt. Crevices such as these may also hide some over-wintering pests such as snails or red spider mites, so use a bristled brush to winkle them out.

In mild weather you may be able to put your plants outside while you clean, perhaps covering them with a couple of layers of horticultural fleece. If this seems a bit risky, simply cram them all together at one end while you tackle the other, then change them round.

TIP
A washing-up brush is ideal for cleaning the outside of the greenhouse, but dislodge any grime in between panes of glass by inserting a thin, flexible plant label and wiggling it about a bit.

Turn up the heat
Time to do: February/March

In early spring a heated propagator is always in demand, even if you keep the greenhouse frost free. The extra heat they offer hugely increases the range of crops you can start off yourself, and means you can get them up and running earlier.

You can sow seed in trays, modular trays, or simply use an ordinary flowerpot in your propagator.

Crops suitable for raising in a heated propagator include chilli peppers, sweet peppers, asparagus, melons, aubergines, greenhouse cucumbers, marrows, tomatoes, courgettes, broccoli and basil.

Peppers and greenhouse tomatoes will really benefit from a heated propagator and should produce a greater crop because the plants will be ready that bit earlier in the year.

For maximum efficiency, keep the propagator in a relatively warm, or at least protected, position. Most entry-level models raise the heat inside the propagator to a fixed point – often 10° to 20°C – above surrounding air temperature. A propagator that allows you to regulate the heat will make life easier, but by simply raising the seed tray or pot off the base of the propagator you can germinate seeds that require a lower temperature.

TIP
To reduce heating costs, make sure the compost is not freezing cold when you sow seed.

STEWART

Get better tomatoes

Tomatoes generally thrive in a warm greenhouse when adequately looked after, but there are also a few tricks of the trade to help produce an even better crop.

When growing tomatoes, regular removal of sideshoots is important to prevent plants from becoming an impenetrable mass of leaves, and it also makes them more productive. This task often worries the less experienced tomato grower, but it is simple: grasp the shoot that appears between the main stem and the leaf with your finger and thumb and bend it sharply downwards. This should give a clean break.

Tomatoes grow best in the greenhouse border, which provides them with a good volume of soil. This makes watering easier, too, because they need watering less often than plants grown in containers or grow bags.

Even in a well-manured border, it's best to provide supplementary feeding because tomatoes thrive on it. Potash, in particular, will help to keep the plants cropping well, and liquid fertilisers specially formulated for tomatoes prove invaluable. The rate and frequency at which these need to be applied varies, so always check the label carefully.

TIP
When removing sideshoots, try not to leave behind a stump that will die back. If your first attempt is not perfect, just pinch out the remains of the shoot and remove it without damaging the adjacent growth.

Don't frazzle in the heat Time to do: spring/summer

From late spring until the end of the summer, temperatures are generally quite high, so it is important to keep the greenhouse well ventilated. This reduces the heat and humidity and ensures a good flow of air around the plants.

Keeping windows open and having plenty of vents mean that bees are able to fly in and out to pollinate the crops, and good air circulation will help keep diseases to a minimum.

An automatic vent is a great help if you're away from home during the day as it will open and close the window, depending on the temperature. Make sure your greenhouse has lots of windows that can be opened and add extra vents if necessary to keep things cool. You can buy easy-to-fit vent kits at good garden centres.

Damping down is a great way to reduce temperatures too. This simply means hosing down the greenhouse floor with cool water. Alternatively, use a watering can. It's best to do it every morning if you can.

If you have them, pull down greenhouse blinds on hotter days, or try adding temporary shading paint to the glass to protect your plants from the sun's scorching summer rays.

TIP
Don't forget that simply opening the door on a hot day is one of the best ways of allowing fresh air to get in and around the greenhouse.

Prolong your peppers

Time to do: autumn

Peppers grown in greenhouses or good-sized cold frames should still be producing plenty of fruits in autumn. Like so many of the other sun lovers, peppers may need much of the summer to really get going, and it is essential that you keep on giving them TLC at this time.

Even inside a greenhouse temperatures will be considerably lower in autumn, so getting the watering regime right can be tricky. Although peppers need a fair amount of moisture, they detest sogginess around their roots. If the compost gets too dry, however, the fruits are likely to develop black bases, which are a sign of blossom end rot, caused by erratic watering. It's a delicate balance.

A plentiful supply of high potash feed is definitely in order. It's best to use the same fertiliser that you give to your tomatoes, and dose them with this every week.

Light levels are lower and the days shorter in autumn, so if there is space on the greenhouse staging, move the peppers in their pots off the greenhouse floor.

TIP
Moving a grow bag full of plants is likely to produce disastrous results, but slipping a rigid board under the full length of the bag makes the task much less risky.

Success with seeds
Time to sow: spring

Spring is the perfect time to sow many vegetable seeds in pots or trays inside, especially tender crops such as courgettes that will need to be raised and grown on outside.

Whatever container you use, make sure it is well scrubbed out before you start, so you don't introduce damping off disease. This common problem causes young seedlings to suddenly collapse and die. Good hygiene is essential to prevent it, and an occasional watering with Cheshunt compound will also help.

Cell or module trays are especially useful for sowing vegetable seeds as they will keep pricking out and transplanting to a minimum.

Sow two seeds per cell as an insurance policy – if both seeds germinate, you can simply weed out the less vigorous seedling early on.

There are many different types of compost available and what you use is up to you, but generally one designed for seed sowing will produce the best results.

TIP
In these days of water shortages, avoid using water from a butt for seedlings. Damping off can be kept at bay by using mains water.

Try biological pest controls

If you're not keen on using chemicals to treat pests and diseases on your fruit and veg, biological controls could be the answer to your problems.

Biological controls work by introducing a large number of natural predators into the greenhouse to attack pests on affected plants. Provided you have suitable conditions, such as adequate temperatures and freedom from any pesticides, these controls really do work.

Some common predators are the parasitic wasp *Encarsia formosa,* used against whitefly; the predatory mite *Phytoseiulus persimilis,* for red spider mite; the nematode *Steinernema kraussei,* for vine weevil; and the ladybird beetle *Cryptolaemus montrouzieri,* used to control mealybugs.

For real success you need to catch the problem before the pest levels have built up, so get your biological controls in place as soon as you spot these fiends.

TIP
Several specialist suppliers offer a mail-order service and will also give you telephone advice to help you tackle your specific problems.

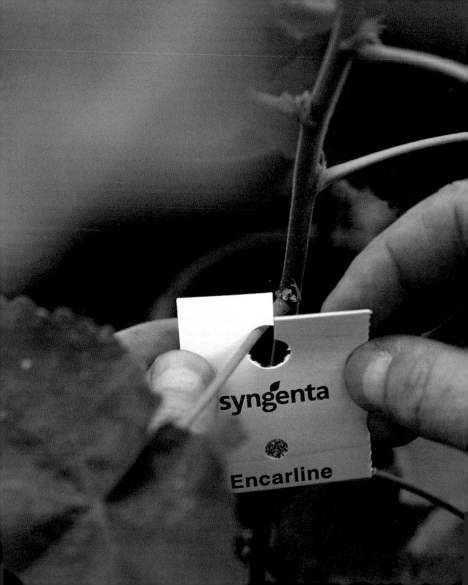

Baskets of early strawberries   Time to plant: spring

One of the advantages of a greenhouse is that you can plant crops such as strawberries sooner than if they were outside, and with just a little heat you can be picking plump, juicy, red fruits a couple of weeks earlier.

If space is at a premium in your greenhouse, why not grow your strawberries in a hanging basket? The natural trailing habit of strawberries makes them ideal for baskets and containers as they tumble over the sides.

You can use any type of basket, as long as it provides a good depth of compost, so that it doesn't dry out too quickly. Add water-retaining crystals to the compost to further reduce the amount of watering needed.

Plants are readily available at garden centres and via mail order from specialist fruit nurseries. Three plants should be about right for a 30–35cm (12–14in) basket. Keep the compost moist at all times and ply with tomato feed and you'll be enjoying fruits before the tennis at Wimbledon.

TIP
Good early-fruiting strawberry varieties are 'Honeoye', 'Elvira' and 'Rosie'.

Cultivate cucumbers

Time to sow: mid- to late spring

Cucumbers are productive plants to grow in a greenhouse and from just one plant you can get upwards of 15 delicious fruits.

As long as you keep cucumbers warm to start with, protect them from scorching with shading paint or netting in hot temperatures, and keep an eye on the watering, they are easy to grow. Fruits should be ready to harvest from midsummer.

It is often said that you cannot grow cucumbers and tomatoes together because they need different growing conditions, but in actual fact they will be quite happy together and should produce a good crop.

Remember that cucumbers don't like draughts while too much moisture around the base of the stems can cause foot and root rots.

Either sow seeds in mid-spring or buy plants in late spring. Plant them on a slightly raised mound of soil to prevent water sitting around the stem. You can also direct water straight to the roots by sinking a flowerpot into the soil alongside the plant and watering into it.

TIP
Cucumbers are climbing plants so they need support as they grow. A piece of trellis is ideal, but canes, wire or twine will do just as well.

Hassle-free watering

Time to do: spring–summer

When the weather is warm, greenhouse plants need watering at least once a day, but this needn't be a hassle if you install an irrigation system to do it for you.

There is a good selection of irrigation systems available, ranging from simple capillary benches to full-blown watering systems controlled by an electronic timer.

A battery-operated timer can be programmed to water several times a day for a set period. Timers can be attached to sprinklers, irrigation systems or soaker hoses.

A dripper system can be the best solution when there are lots of different plants spread around the greenhouse.

A kit comes with drippers, sprinklers and clips. Once set up, simply adjust the flow of water according to the weather conditions.

To water hanging baskets, containers or grow bags, a simple dripper system can be run from a large water-filled bag. A short length of tube will slowly deliver the water to your plants.

TIP
Install an irrigation system before you go away on holiday and you can leave the greenhouse to look after itself rather than having to ask friends and neighbours to pop in and water.

Juicy peaches

Time to plant: late autumn–early spring

Peaches are one of the most delicious summer fruits but are often thought too exotic to grow in Britain. In fact, they are totally hardy, but because they blossom early in the season the flowers can be damaged by frosts.

Although they can be grown outside in a sheltered position, peaches will crop more reliably in a greenhouse. A cold greenhouse will offer just enough protection in early spring when the blossom is produced and will also stop the fungus that causes peach leaf curl from attacking the plant.

The easiest way to grow peaches is in a fan shape, either on a wall or at the end of a greenhouse. The size of the fan will depend on space, but an established plant that is 1.8m (6ft) wide will produce a crop of around 40 peaches.

Establishing the basic framework of a fan does take one or two growing seasons, depending on the age of the tree that you buy, but after that period, pruning and other maintenance are very easy. You will also need to hand pollinate flowers with a brush and then thin out any fruits as they appear.

TIP
Try 'Peregrine', with white flesh; 'Rochester', a reliable cropper; and 'Duke of York', which has an intense flavour.

Take cuttings Time to do: spring–summer

Buying plants can be a costly business, so take a few cuttings of your favourite herbs to get extra ones for free.

The best time of year to take cuttings is spring or summer, when the plant has plenty of new, leafy growth.

Select a healthy shoot that doesn't have any flowers – such as the sprig of apple mint pictured. Make a sloping cut with a sharp pair of scissors or a knife, just under a pair of leaves. Remove the bottom leaves, as these would rot if left on when the cutting goes into the compost.

Mix perlite or grit into a multi-purpose compost, to make it free-draining, and fill a module tray or pots. Use a dibber or pencil to make a hole in the compost and insert the cutting. Gently firm it in.

Water the cuttings and place them on a well-lit windowsill. Plant the cuttings out into individual pots when they have rooted.

TIP
Rosemary, mint, thyme and sage are ideal herbs for propagation by cuttings. If you have any spares, swap them with friends and family to fill your herb garden.

Successional herbs

To have a constant supply of herbs that will add zing to your cooking or your salads, ditch those short-lived plants from the supermarket and sow your own.

Tender and fast-germinating annual herbs such as basil and coriander are a must in warmer weather, and if you sow pots of seed regularly from spring onwards you should have a supply all summer.

Sow the seeds thinly onto moist compost, sieve a little more compost over the top and pop the pots into a heated propagator or onto a warm windowsill.

Move them into bigger pots outside as soon as the seedlings appear, then grow them on until they're ready for snipping. It's as easy as that.

TIP
Keep sowing small quantities of seeds and you'll always have your favourite, super-fresh herbs to hand.

Plant great garlic

Time to plant: spring or autumn

Garlic is an essential ingredient in so many dishes, so it's brilliant to have your own supply just outside the kitchen door.

Garlic thrives in a sunny spot in well-drained soil, but it will also grow in heavier soils provided the drainage is improved. This is easily done by planting the bulbs on a 13–15cm (5–6in) high ridge of soil and adding grit if necessary.

You can plant garlic bulbs in spring, but planting in autumn will achieve the largest, plumpest and earliest crop. When planting, split the bulbs into cloves and space them 15cm (6in) apart, with 30cm (1ft) between rows.

Order bulbs from a seed catalogue, as they are generally the best quality. A good variety is 'Vitesse', which has a beautiful purple-pink flush and is ready by early June. It is also wonderfully tasty when harvested a few weeks early and stores for four or five months. 'Ivory' is also good; it is a pure white variety ready by mid-July. Its real asset, apart from its wonderful taste and aroma, is that it stores until late spring.

TIP

Only plant garlic that has been specifically produced for growing and is certified virus and eelworm free. Using leftovers from your vegetable rack is likely to result in virus problems.

Freeze fresh herbs

Time to do: summer–autumn

During the summer and early autumn many herbs put on a phenomenal amount of growth, and supply can outstrip demand. Drying is the traditional method of preserving herbs, but freezing them is also well worth trying.

A whole range of delicious herbs can be frozen successfully, including parsley, basil, thyme, oregano and chives.

Select only the healthiest, freshest shoots and cut them off cleanly. Wash, then carefully chop into small pieces. Pour water into an ice-cube tray, filling it a quarter full, then pack each cube with the chopped herbs, ensuring that as much of the leaf as possible is covered by water. Top up the tray with water to just below the rim.

Put the tray in the freezer, keeping it level, and leave it to freeze. This method ensures they hold onto their flavour because they are frozen when fresh.

These herbs are now easy to use: when a recipe requires a particular herb, simply take a cube or two and pop it straight into your saucepan. Drop these herbs into casseroles and sauces while they are cooking, and as the ice melts, your dishes are infused with the delicious flavour of home-grown herbs.

TIP
Save yourself time and hassle – decant the frozen cubes into labelled bags and put them back into the freezer. Then when you need a herb you know exactly where it is and can take it straight out of the bag.

Try something different

Rosemary is an interesting herb in its own right – it looks lovely, smells marvellous and tastes great. It is also an evergreen plant.

There are some lovely varieties to look out for, one of the better known ones is *Rosmarinus officinalis* 'Miss Jessopp's Upright', which has pale blue flowers and a very upright habit. If you fancy another colour rather than blue, then there is a white-flowered form, *R. officinalis* var. *albiflorus*, or you could try the pink-flowered *R. officinalis* 'Roseus' or 'Majorca Pink'.

It is not only the flowers that can vary, but also the growth habit of the plants. *R. officinalis* Prostratus Group is a trailing variety that has pale blue flowers, while the stunning, blue *R. officinalis* 'Fota Blue' has arching stems.

The scent of the leaves can also vary. *R. officinalis* var. *angustissimus* 'Benenden Blue', for example, has a very piney scent, while *R. officinalis* 'Green Ginger', as its name suggests, has a hint of ginger.

TIP
Visit a specialist herb nursery to see – and smell – the full spectrum of varieties.

Divide herbs Time to do: spring or autumn

An easy way to increase the quantity of herb plants, including oregano and mint, is to divide an established clump.

To divide a herb, simply dig up the parent plant and split it into pieces, each with its own roots and leaves.

Some plants can simply be pulled apart, such as the oregano pictured, but others are harder to break up. If that's the case, either insert two garden forks back to back in the centre of the clump and lever them apart, or get an old bread knife or a pruning saw and cut through the clump. It may look brutal, but the plant will soon recover.

Replant the new pieces as soon as possible after the plant is split. Alternatively, pot them up until you're ready to put them in the ground. Keep them well-watered for the first few months after planting while they establish new roots. The new plants will soon put on growth until they are eventually big enough to be split apart themselves.

TIP
This technique can be used with many ornamental plants as well, such as hostas and phlox.

The secret of sowing parsley

Parsley is one of those all-round useful plants that no fully functioning herb garden should be without. There are many superstitions associated with sowing parsley, but it's really not that tricky to grow a good crop.

The most important factor in sowing parsley seeds is not to allow them to dry out during germination. If sown in early spring under protection – at around 18°C (65°F) – germination should take two to four weeks. Alternatively, sow the seed in a prepared site in late spring when the night temperature does not fall below 7°C (45°F). Seeds should germinate in two to four weeks.

Parsley is a hungry plant that likes a good deep soil, not too light and not acidic. Always feed the chosen site with well-rotted manure in the previous autumn.

Parsley is ideal for container growing, and it should thrive indoors on a windowsill as long as it is watered, fed and cut regularly. You could also try growing it in a hanging basket, but it must be kept well watered. Alternatively, try it in a window box, but do give it some shade in high summer. When growing parsley in a container, allow enough room for the tap root to develop.

TIP
Parsley makes an ideal companion plant when sown with vegetables. It is said to keep onion fly away and to deter carrot root flies. Parsley also grows well with tomatoes and will flourish when sharing their feed.

Know your tarragon

There are three herbs commonly called tarragon – all are herbaceous, have mid-green narrow leaves and a distinctive aniseed flavour.

The Rolls-Royce of tarragon is the French one, *Artemisia dracunculus*, with its distinctive aniseed flavour that is renowned in Béarnaise sauce and chicken and tarragon dishes. French tarragon can transform roast chicken into a feast and makes soups and sauces a digestive delight.

Russian tarragon, *Artemisia dracunculus* subsp. *dracunculoides*, has long oval leaves with a slightly bitter flavour and only a hint of aniseed; it is commonly used in Persia as a salad plant. It is very hardy and has attractive sprays of tiny yellow blooms in summer.

Winter tarragon, *Tagetes lucida*, is from Mexico and has coarser, larger leaves than its cousins. It dies back in spring rather than winter, hence its common name. Winter tarragon has a very strong aniseed flavour and so it is better used in cooked dishes, especially with roast meat or vegetables and in soups.

TIP
French tarragon is the only type worth preserving. The quickest and easiest method is to make an infusion with fresh leaves and white wine vinegar, which can then be used to make salad dressings and sauces.

Sow herbs in a grow bag

Time to sow: May–Sept

Grow bags are generally associated with greenhouse crops such as tomatoes and sweet peppers, but they are also great for growing herbs.

Leaf crops grow best when positioned in partial shade, as this prevents the leaves scorching in the midday sun. It also helps stop the grow bag from drying out. (There should be instructions on the bag about making holes for drainage.)

Cut two large windows in the plastic to give you the maximum sowing area for your crops. Once the bag is opened, use a fork to fluff up the compost. Water the bag well, then use a pencil or length of dowel, pressed horizontally into the compost, to mark out your sowing lines. In a standard-size bag you can have up to six rows.

May is the ideal time to start sowing outside, and you can continue sowing until early September.

To guarantee pickings over the winter months, put the grow bag in a cold greenhouse from September onwards.

TIP
Tape the grow bag in the middle prior to cutting – this will give it extra strength when you cut the openings.

Growing mint

Time to plant: spring–autumn

One of the most popular of all herbs is mint. It has been used for hundreds of years to flavour food, sweets, toothpaste and medicines and comes in a tempting array of flavours and forms.

Mint can be used fresh, scattered over green or fruit salads, or chopped up and added to mayonnaise or salad dressing. It can also be cooked with vegetables such as peas to bring them to life. Alternatively, use it to add a heavenly minty flavour to chocolate mousse.

Some particularly flavoursome varieties include mild-flavoured gingermint, *Mentha* x *gracilis* 'Variegata', which has gold and green leaves, chocolate peppermint, *M.* x *piperita* f. *citrata* 'Chocolate', which has dark brown leaves that taste rather like After Eights, and red mint, *M.* x *smithiana*, with red stems and green and brown tinted leaves that have a good spearmint flavour.

Renowned for being invasive, you should plant mint with care. The best-flavoured and healthiest plants are those that spread naturally, so plant them in a rich, well-drained soil, in a sunny spot where they can grow unrestricted. If space is an issue, plant mint in containers to control it. However, plants can die in pots, so to prevent the roots rotting, repot every autumn using a soil-based compost.

TIP
Cut back hard after flowering for a fresh supply of leaves in early autumn.

Save your seed

Saving seeds from your herbs is an easy way to enjoy home-grown plants – it is great fun and very rewarding, both inspirationally and financially.

Late summer and early autumn are the ideal times to start collecting seeds. By then many plants have produced seed heads that are becoming brown and dry, and this is their signal to you that they are ripe.

Choose a dry, preferably sunny, day, so the seeds are as dry as possible. Arm yourself with either brown paper envelopes or boxes lined with paper or kitchen towel (to absorb any moisture), sticky labels and a pencil.

Remove the whole seed head using secateurs or scissors, but don't snap it off because this can cause you to lose a lot of seeds. Collect seeds in separate envelopes or boxes, taking care not to mix them up. Seeds encased in berries should be collected as soon as the berries are just over-ripe.

TIP
It's easy to forget which seeds are which by the time you get indoors, so label them as you go. Add the date before storing, so that you know how old they are and whether they are still viable when you come to sow them.

Time to harvest

Harvesting herbs regularly not only benefits us, but it also helps keep the plants productive and healthy. However, there's a right and a wrong way to harvest them, so to get the most from your herbs it pays to know how they grow.

Herbs grow in one of two ways: by producing leaves along a stem, or by shooting stems up from the base or crown. Stem-grown plants include bay, thyme and mint, while crown-forming examples are chives, parsley and rocket.

These leafy herbs should be nipped off where the leaf meets the stem, while crown-forming herbs should be taken right back to near the base of the stems using scissors or a knife – think of it as pruning on a small scale. Get it right and you'll have sturdy, long-lasting plants that will keep you supplied all summer. Get it wrong, and it's goodbye to your crops.

To harvest successfully you need to know how to pick herbs, and also when to do it. For those with succulent leaves, such as basil, pick before flowers are formed. Once this process starts, all the plant's energy goes into producing blooms and then seed, and the leaves become tough and sour.

For evergreen herbs such as sage, cut off the flowers and give the plant a good trim in late summer for a second flush of leaves that will provide you with succulent pickings through autumn and winter.

TIP
Harvest annuals such as parsley before they run to seed; after this they won't produce any new leaves.

Make a bouquet garni

There is nothing more comforting on a cold winter's day than tucking into a casserole that has been cooked with fresh herbs. This is how food used to be enjoyed, and so it can be today.

By using fresh herbs in your cooking, you can create a wonderful and healthy meal, and key to these dishes is the bouquet garni, which means 'a bunch of flavouring herbs'. These are commonly used to enhance the flavour of soups and casseroles, which are usually cooked in a single pot.

The origins of the bouquet garni can be traced back to medieval times when meals were cooked in a pot over an open fire and the green vegetables were known as 'pot herbs'. A few herbs still retain the name 'pot' in their common name, such as pot marjoram, *Origanum vulgare*.

A mixture of herbs, including bay, lemon thyme, lemon balm, lemon grass leaves, rosemary, summer savory, hyssop, thyme, tarragon and parsley, is excellent with chicken. Or use any combination of fennel, lemon balm, French parsley, mint, sweet marjoram, tarragon, a small sprig of lovage, dill, Welsh onion stems and bay with fish. If you want to flavour a meat-based casserole, then try using a selection of oregano, thyme, bay, lovage, rosemary, sage or parsley.

TIP
Use a long piece of undyed string to tie your herbs together, as this makes it easy to remove the bouquet garni at the end of cooking.

Herbs for shade
Time to plant: spring–autumn

It's a generally held belief that herbs prefer full sun, especially the Mediterranean types such as thyme, sage and oregano. However, herbs such as chervil (pictured), parsley, salad rocket and coriander actually benefit from being grown in partial shade.

Herbs that prefer shady conditions are happier there because they hate the soil drying out in summer. They produce better leaf crops if they're not subjected to the midday sun and, because the soil doesn't dry out as rapidly, they're less prone to bolt (flower quickly) and will therefore continue to produce leaves for a longer length of time.

Keeping such herbs in partial shade can result in softer leaves that have a more subtle flavour. This is a real advantage with some herbs, such as sorrel, which becomes tough and bitter when it is grown in full sun. On the other hand, shade is not good for mint or chives, as it can cause them to grow leggy. If you regularly cut their leaves, you can keep them under control and encourage them to produce new growth.

TIP
Avoid growing sweet marjoram, summer savory and cardoon in shade. They grow so weakly in cool spots that they keel over and become food for slugs and snails.

Growing supermarket basil   Time to plant: spring

Basil is definitely one of the most rewarding herbs to grow. It's an attractive plant that comes in many shapes, sizes and colours, and is grown all over the world.

There are many types of basil, all of which are edible, and all have a different flavour. It's a wonderful culinary herb and its versatility in the kitchen is matched in the garden, where striking purple basils make superb spot plants at the front of a warm border.

All basils make excellent companion plants, and the reliable bush varieties are great planted throughout the vegetable garden, as they repel a number of pests.

Supermarket basil is raised quickly (22 days from seed to sale), so the rootball is underdeveloped compared to conventionally raised plants. This is why supermarket basil (the left-hand plant in the picture, alongside a home-grown basil) normally dies if it is planted out in the garden. If you want to keep supermarket herbs going, divide them with care and repot in light compost. Keep the compost moist but don't let it dry out. Place in a warm position until the plants are fully rooted. They should then grow on like seed-raised basil.

TIP
Basil is known for repelling house flies, so it's ideal for growing in containers positioned outside your kitchen door.

Make more of your crop

Freezing and drying work well as ways of preserving herbs for use later in the year, but to get a little something extra from them, try making herb butters and vinegars to capture the delicious taste of fresh herbs.

To make a herb vinegar, pick lots of sprigs of your favourite herbs and submerge them in as big a drum of white wine vinegar as you can get your hands on. It's best to blanch them first (plunge the sprigs into a mug of boiling water to kill any possible bugs), then leave them to steep for a month in the vinegar before straining.

Herb butters also make great use of any excess harvest. To make a butter, take a good handful of any soft green herb, such as chives, tarragon and parsley, and add it to two pats of soft butter, mixing it all together in a food processor. Remove the mix, place it on some cling film, roll it into a cylinder and freeze. Cut off discs as and when you want them to put on top of steaks or carrots.

TIP
Herb butters and vinegars are incredibly useful in flavouring a wide range of dishes, and a bottle of homemade vinegar is a perfect present.

Make a lavender bath bag   Time to do: summer

Herbs can affect the mind and emotions in ways we are only just beginning to understand. Anyone who has had aromatherapy treatment knows how relaxing, stimulating or uplifting it can be – and this is down to the fragrance as well as the absorption of the oil.

Lavender is one of the most useful herbs to aid relaxation. Not only is it generally regarded as a tonic for the nervous system, it is also a potent sedative and calming remedy. Lavender is particularly effective in helping to relax you and soothe your nerves when added to a bath – as a few drops of lavender oil or as fresh or dried lavender flowers.

To make a lavender bath bag, place a handful of dried blooms in a square of muslin. Take the four corners of the muslin and tie them together securely with string. Make a loop to hang it from the bath tap. Allow the hot water to run through the bag. This will not only scent the water, but will also fragrance the whole room.

TIP

The fragrance of lavender produces a calming response, so plant it beneath windows or around seating areas. Then you can sit, breathe it in and exhale gently at times of stress or at the end of a long day.

Soothe the skin   Time to plant: all year round

Using plants directly on the skin to ease pain or treat surface ailments is an age-old practice – and a very effective one. So why not grow your own natural remedies and have a pharmacy on your doorstep?

Aloe vera is a remarkable plant for its healing powers, both internally and externally. In the 1930s, research looked into the properties of the gel that is produced when a leaf is broken, and a chemical was found that stimulates the immune system. However, *Aloe vera* is most commonly known to soothe burns – the gel forms a protective seal over the wound and helps the skin to heal beneath it. It is also beneficial for fungal infections such as ringworm, as well as minor cases of sunburn and eczema.

Pot marigold petals are antiseptic, while the plant's other healing properties help to prevent the spread of infection. A cream made from the petals also makes an excellent remedy for sore or inflamed skin.

Oil made from the flowers of St John's wort can be applied to nerve-damaged skin in conditions such as shingles, rashes and minor burns, to help it regenerate. Don't use it too often, though, as excessive use can cause the skin to become very sensitive to light and make it prone to sunburn.

TIP
Keep an *Aloe vera* plant in the kitchen, so whenever you burn yourself you can break off a piece of leaf and apply the gel to the wound.

Make a herbal tea

As we all try to reduce our caffeine intake, we are advised to drink herbal teas. Try a cup of your own home-grown herb tea and you'll be amazed at the flavours.

Next time you feel bloated after a meal or have an attack of indigestion, try a cup of peppermint tea. Simply put a handful of fresh or dried leaves into a teapot or mug, pour over boiling water and allow it to stand for five minutes with a lid on. It's important to keep it covered because the evaporating steam carries the essential oil. When you drink it, the warmth, flavours and aromas of the tea help you to relax, while also easing that bloated feeling.

A cup of fennel seed tea can ease the pain when you are suffering from wind or stomach cramps. Place one teaspoon of seeds in a teacup, pour over boiling water, let it stand, then strain and drink. Fennel seeds are also very beneficial when chewed after a rich or spicy meal, as they help freshen the breath and settle the stomach.

A tea made from hyssop leaves is an excellent tonic if you are suffering from a cough and cold, as it is a gentle decongestant and expectorant. However, avoid drinking it if you are pregnant.

TIP
If you're suffering from the effects of the night before and have a big day ahead of you, brew yourself a cup of fresh rosemary tea – it helps to stimulate the memory and clear a hangover.

Early salads under cover

Time to plant: late winter/early spring

Supermarkets sell a wide range of salad leaves, but you'll find that few are organically grown and they are often not as fresh as they might be, so it is far better to grow your own.

Provided light levels are high enough, it is worth growing a few lettuces or salad-leaf plants in your greenhouse in late winter and early spring or under a mini-tunnel made of polythene or fleece, bought at any garden centre.

If your greenhouse has soil-filled borders, grow salad leaves before crops such as tomatoes are planted, then later you can fit them in among the crops. Cover salad plants to encourage rapid growth and earlier cropping. You could use fleece or mini-cloches, but individual bell cloches seem to work best. Choose ones with a vent in the top, so there is good air circulation.

Covering plants also helps to protect them from slugs and snails, which find the succulent young leaves as irresistible as we do.

TIP
There's a great selection of salad seeds available, including special mixtures. However, if you have favourite types of salad, it's worth buying individual packets and combining them into your own mix.

Protect salads from slugs

Time to do: spring

Slugs seem to be addicted to salads and can munch through whole crops in one sitting. In a warm, damp year the problem can become so bad that it starts to feel personal!

Lettuces are the salad crop most susceptible to slugs and snails, so it's worth starting a few plants off in pots inside before planting them out. This way they are that little bit bigger, tougher and slightly less desirable to munch on than the younger seedlings.

Sow the seeds on the surface of the compost in spring and keep them under cover for a few weeks, preferably in a greenhouse. As the weather improves, move them out to a cold frame to harden them off for the great outdoors.

Don't be tempted to pop freshly sown seeds in a heated propagator to speed things up, as high temperatures actually slow down and often even prevent germination of lettuce seeds. That's why lettuces sown in the heat of summer often fail to appear.

TIP
Gardeners have found that lettuces with red in the leaves, such as 'Lollo Rossa' and 'Revolution', seem to be less attractive to slugs.

Grow rocket from seed

Time to sow: March–September

Rocket has shot up fast in the trendy-eating stakes – everyone seems to love its spicy, almost peppery flavour. Better still, it is very easy to grow.

A single packet of seeds is usually enough to sow a row 3–6m (10–20ft) long, depending on the variety of rocket you choose. There are always plenty of seeds in a packet. Ideally, use just a small quantity at one go.

Sow a pinch of seeds every few weeks and as each plant finishes another will be ready for cropping. That way you will be able to harvest the delicious leaves over a longer period.

The only real problem you'll have with rocket is the flea beetle, which eats the leaves, biting out tiny circular holes. If you sow seed in summer, the flea beetle will be particularly troublesome. The simple solution is to cover the row with a length of horticultural fleece or a fleece-covered mini-tunnel. You should get a perfect-looking and fine-tasting harvest within weeks.

TIP
Rocket is best sown between March and September, but later sowings will reward you with a good crop of surprisingly tender leaves.

Ripen the last tomatoes

Time to do: September–October

If the last tomato fruits are still hanging off your plants in autumn, then with light and temperature levels falling, it's time to give nature a helping hand.

If you are happy to maintain plants a little longer, any extra weather protection you can give will help, so towards the end of September or in early October lay outdoor tomato plants gently onto a thick mat of straw and cover them with a cloche. Any miserable, drawn plants that you have left are ready for the compost heap.

Rather than waste the remaining fruits, pick them off and place them in a paper bag with an overripe banana – choose the freckled and squidgy sort left in the bottom of the fruit bowl. The ethylene gas given off by this banana acts as a natural ripening agent and turns green tomatoes red. The end result is probably a lot more appealing than yet another batch of green tomato chutney.

TIP
You can still rescue and lay down tomato plants well into the autumn by covering them with a layer or two of loosely draped fleece.

Compost bags as growing bags

Even gardeners with lots of open ground often opt to raise their tomatoes in grow bags, but it can be more effective to use bags of compost instead.

Growing bags can work well, although keeping plants adequately moist can be quite a challenge, because the volume of compost is relatively small, and it can be hard to re-wet if allowed to dry out. To get around this problem, use a bag of regular compost instead; the larger volume of compost makes life a lot easier.

Plant out your tomatoes when they are about 15cm (6in) tall. Water the plants in their pots half an hour before you transplant them. Shake the bag to break up any large clumps of compost and, using a sharp knife, remove a rectangle of plastic from one face of the bag. Fluff up the compost further with a hand fork or trowel, then dig the first planting hole, making it a bit larger than the plant pot.

Ease the plant from its pot. Cradle its rootball, supporting the plant's stem with your fingers. Place the young plant in its hole with the rootball just beneath the compost's surface and firm it in. Repeat, putting three plants in each bag. Stab small holes in the base for drainage, then water well.

TIP
Buy a good quality compost for your tomatoes, but whatever you buy will usually be better quality than many growing bags available.

When to water

Salads are made up of a high proportion of water, which is what gives them wonderful crisp and juicy textures. To enjoy the best tasting salads, it's essential to get their watering right.

Wherever possible, water in the evening, as watering in the heat of the day will result in a lot of moisture being lost through evaporation. This means that your plants will not get what they need, so you are wasting your time and energy.

Larger plants, such as tomatoes, benefit from having a plant pot sunk into the ground alongside them. Filling this with water means it will go direct to the roots, thus decreasing loss by run off.

Lay a seep hose or irrigation dripper and set it to deliver the water to a large area at a turn of the tap.

Covering the pipes with a mulch will help to avoid water being lost through evaporation, as will mulching the soil surface around the plants.

TIP
Watering on soft foliage during periods of bright sunlight is more likely to cause scorching, so water on dull days or wait until evening.

Grow lettuce Time to sow: spring–autumn

Lettuce seedlings are a delicious feast for slugs and snails, so give yourself a chance to eat your own lettuce plants by raising the seeds indoors and transplanting them when they are bigger and stronger.

Where you sow lettuce seeds is important, as they don't tend to germinate in high temperatures. Above 21°C (70°F) the rate of germination drops dramatically, so bear this in mind when deciding whether to sow indoors or in the open ground.

Cell or module trays work particularly well for lettuces, as you won't have to prick out the seedlings. Sow three or four seeds per cell, then thin them out to leave the two healthiest-looking seedlings. A week or so later, thin them out to the sturdiest plant in each cell.

Plants grown in cells or modules also have well-developed root systems when you plant them out. This means they can grow on happily without getting too big for their pots, so the timings for planting out don't have to be so precise.

Water them in after planting and they will grow at a rate of knots. Larger young plants are usually less subject to the vagaries of the weather than transplanted seedlings, and are better able to fight off pests and diseases than those sown direct in the ground.

TIP
Sow inside the greenhouse in spring and autumn, and sow into a cold frame or cloche when the weather is warmer.

When to harvest   Time to do: late spring–autumn

The high water content of most salads means that in hot weather you'll notice a difference in the succulence of your salads according to the time of day they are picked. So when is the best time to harvest?

Salad crops are best picked in the early morning, before they experience the dehydrating effects of the sun. Alternatively, give the plants a thorough drenching and then harvest them a few hours later, once they've had a chance to absorb the water.

However, you will get the strongest flavour from tomatoes if they are harvested before watering, because water is absorbed quickly by the plant and a recent drenching will reduce the intensity of the tomatoes' flavour.

Bear in mind, too, when harvesting salads, that younger leaves tend to be crisper and tastier than older ones. Plants with heads of leaves, such as lettuces, are best if the older, outer leaves are removed, leaving only the young, tasty ones.

TIP
Don't store damaged crops, as they will not last as long as perfect ones. Instead use them as soon as you've picked them, eating them raw or cooking them in a sauce.

Tasty winter salads

Time to sow: September

There's nothing like the taste of home-grown salads, and even when summer's over, you can still enjoy fresh pickings.

Sow a selection of lettuce and salad leaves in September and you'll be harvesting from autumn to spring. The earlier you sow, the sooner you'll be picking, so don't delay. For best results, sowings should be completed by mid- to late September.

Although the range of lettuce and salad leaf varieties for September sowing isn't as wide as it is for spring sowing, most seed companies offer a good selection. When choosing varieties, select hardy types, as they'll cope with the harsh winter conditions. Many summer salads simply won't tolerate the cold and wet of a typical winter outside.

There are two ways you can grow winter salads. The first is to simply sow the seeds directly outside. The second is to raise young plants in pots or modules, then plant them out later. Whichever method you choose, remember to pick a warm, sheltered site. Light and warmth are crucial for successful winter salad crops, and the protection of a cloche is vital through the winter months.

TIP

Good salad crops to sow in September include cut-and-come-again varieties of lettuce, wild rocket, mizuna and corn salad (sometimes sold as lamb's lettuce).

Try sprouting seeds

Time to sow: any time of year

Most people think of bean sprouts as the long, white mung bean sprouts traditionally used in Chinese cooking. But there is a wide range of sprouting seeds, including sunflower, onion and basil, each with their own distinct flavour.

Sprouting seeds are delicious raw in salads or cooked in stir-fries, and are highly nutritious. Best of all, they're extremely easy to grow. All you need is a jam jar, water and a piece of muslin, and seeds are ready to eat in about a week. You can buy the seeds at the garden centre or by mail order.

To sprout the seeds, put a handful of seeds in a jar and cover well with water. Place a piece of muslin over the top of the jar and leave the seeds to soak overnight. The next morning, drain the water out through the muslin, rinse the seeds in fresh water and drain again, then place the jar on its side. Rinse the seeds at least twice daily through the muslin cloth until the sprouts are ready to eat. Rinse the sprouts again before eating.

Good seeds to try include: lentil sprouts – a member of the pea family, they have a nutty flavour; the colourful shoots of beet, which are perfect for salads and have a delicate beetroot taste; and spring onions, which have a mild onion flavour that makes them ideal for salads or sandwiches.

TIP

A good kids' gardening project is to get them sprouting alfalfa seeds. They are among the fastest to grow, and the sprouts are usually ready within two to four days.

Grow watercress
Time to sow: spring–autumn

You don't need a stream or a pond to grow watercress successfully. It's easy to raise from seed and will provide crops of delicious leaves all summer.

Sowing watercress is simple – it will easily germinate in pots, just like mustard and cress. Either raise indoors or sow direct outside, in a shady place, from mid-May to September.

To sow indoors, fill some small pots with compost, sprinkle the seeds over the surface and water well. Seeds germinate readily in a couple of weeks. Keep watered and place in good light.

Once the seedlings have developed good root systems, split them into small clumps and transplant into larger pots. Water regularly and check the pots to make sure they're kept moist at all times. In four to six weeks, the watercress will be ready to harvest.

Regular harvesting will encourage the plants to keep producing fresh leaves. These spicy-tasting leaves are packed with calcium and iron, making them a great addition to a healthy diet.

TIP
A good variety to try is 'Aqua', which is available from mail-order seed companies.

Sow salads in guttering

Time to sow: spring

Trying out new ways to sow and grow crops is not only fun, but can lead to greater success than more conventional methods.

Sowing salads in guttering indoors and then transplanting them outside produces more reliable results than sowing outdoors. All you need to do is cut a length of plastic guttering into short sections and fill each one with peat-free compost, stopping just short of the ends. Firm it down gently, so that it's level with the rim.

Space the seeds evenly along the length of the guttering, in rows. Keep them in an unheated greenhouse and the seeds should germinate in about a week.

When the seedlings are ready to plant out, dig a shallow trench across your vegetable beds to the depth of your guttering. Test it for size with the piece of guttering, without removing the plants. Once the site is prepared, gently slide the whole row of salad plants and compost straight out of the guttering and into the trench. Break it into shorter sections if this is easier.

Water the salads really well to settle their roots into their new home.

TIP
This technique also works brilliantly with peas.

Get ahead with potatoes

Time to do: January–March

The very mention of chitting potatoes may fill less experienced gardeners with dread, as it makes the whole process sound frighteningly technical. But it's actually a simple, straightforward task, and just requires a few old egg boxes or seed trays.

'Chitting' simply means you give seed potatoes a chance to produce a few good, sturdy shoots before you put them in the ground. This should in turn result in a heavier, and slightly earlier, crop.

Allow four to six weeks for chitting, so that the shoots are about 2cm (¾in) long at planting time. It is an especially beneficial exercise for early varieties, because it can produce a crop that is ready anything up to three weeks sooner.

Decide how many tubers you need and set them in egg boxes, seed trays or similar. A quick glance at each tuber should reveal which way up to place them. The uppermost end should bear more of the nascent shoots (the 'eyes') and will be slightly blunt.

Label each variety and place them in a cool frost-free spot with plenty of natural light.

TIP
Chitting will achieve the best results at a temperature of 7°C (45°F), so leaving them on a cool windowsill is ideal.

Bigger, better onions   Time to do: spring–summer

Onions are particularly vulnerable to competition from weeds. That's because onion plants provide very little leaf cover to shade the ground around them and prevent weeds sprouting. But there are ways to defend your onions and beat the weeds.

Most soils seem to play host to a good supply of weeds, especially if they have been well-manured. A well-nourished soil will provide perfect conditions for weeds, as well as for your crops, and can mean they grow extremely fast and cause a lot of competition.

Regular weeding is essential to produce healthy crops. If you let weeds get established, they will certainly reduce air circulation around onion plants. However, removing well-established weeds is more likely to disturb the onions, so it's probably best to just hoe off the tops.

Weeding by hand around onions and garlic works well, as you can pull out any deep-rooted perennials and hoe off any sprouting annual weeds. On a hot day you could leave annual weeds on the soil surface to dry up and die, but otherwise put them on the compost heap. It is important to remove the old weeds in order to avoid increasing the moisture levels in the air, which can lead to downy mildew disease.

TIP
An onion hoe is perfect for hoeing off weeds – its small head fits neatly between the rows of swelling bulbs, and it's easy to manoeuvre without damaging the crops.

Outdoor aubergines

Time to plant: June

Aubergines need plenty of bright sunshine to do well, far more than crops such as tomatoes and sweet peppers, so you need to plant them where they can bask in maximum sunlight.

Aubergines enjoying growing in a greenhouse, but don't despair if you don't have one as they are happy outside too, as long as they're given a bit of extra protection, such as polythene covers. A great advantage with plants that are grown outside is that they don't tend to suffer from whitefly, a pest that can get to plague-like proportions in a greenhouse.

You'll find plenty of young aubergine plants at garden centres in late spring, ready to plant outside after last frosts. Put them into large pots or grow bags for harvesting from late summer onwards. Towards late autumn the plants do need extra protection, but you can still collect fruits from plants grown under polythene covers after the first frosts.

Feed aubergine plants in the same way that you would tomatoes, using a high-potash liquid tomato fertiliser to encourage good flowers and fruit.

TIP
Aubergines hate having their feet too wet, so keep their soil or compost just moist at all times.

Make onions last   Time to do: mid summer

Years ago, everyone used to suggest speeding up the ripening process of onions by bending the foliage over at the neck. Few people do this now, believing that it is far better to gently but firmly lift each bulb slightly with a fork, so breaking the roots.

This gentle method works well as long you wait until the foliage is just starting to yellow naturally in mid summer. If the weather happens to be unusually wet when you want to harvest your onions, you can lift the bulbs when the leaves are still green. However, as soon as the foliage is definitely on the turn to yellow, remove the bulbs completely from the soil and leave them on their sides to dry off in the summer sunshine.

If there is any chance of more than a very brief shower, then transfer the onions to a sheltered spot. A cold frame is good, but anywhere will do as long as it is well ventilated, light and warm.

Once the onions are dry, they can be stored in net bags or old tights. Alternatively, plait the foliage together to make a traditional onion string.

TIP
It is essential to get the more moist, root-end of the bulbs clear of the soil for them to dry rapidly and thoroughly, so always give them plenty of space when you lay them out.

Make space for courgettes

Time to sow: mid-spring

Picked when really young and tender, courgettes are excellent for cooking, stir-frying and adding to salads. Reckon on getting at least a dozen courgettes off a single plant, so they're a great use of space.

Courgettes are one of the easiest vegetables to grow. Like many crops, the more regularly you harvest them, the more fruits form.

Many people prefer the green-skinned varieties such as 'Defender' and 'Zucchini', because they're heavier croppers and their skins can be more tender than the yellow varieties such as 'Gold Rush' and 'Taxi'.

If you like experimenting with different varieties, try a few of the spherical courgettes such as 'Leprechaun' as well. Harvest these when they are very tender, slightly larger than a tennis ball. Slice the top off, scoop out some of the flesh and you have a courgette perfect for stuffing.

The huge bright yellow flowers of any type of courgette are also a real delicacy. In smart restaurants you occasionally find them lightly coated in batter and deep fried, or stuffed with ricotta cheese. Harvesting the flowers, still perky and intact, is easy when you grow your own.

TIP
Courgettes are ready to pick as soon as they are anything upwards of the thickness of your thumb.

Prevent carrot problems

Time to sow: spring–summer

Freshly pulled, given a rinse and crunched without delay is the best way to eat carrots, but the thought of ones that are tunnelled by maggots is very unappetising.

Carrot fly larvae can be a real problem and prevention is the only solution.

There are resistant varieties available, such as 'Sytan' and 'Flyaway', which work well, but not everyone enjoys their flavour. Instead, it's best to grow classic varieties such as 'Amsterdam Forcing 3' and 'Nantes' under protection. To do this, make a simple wooden frame about 60cm (2ft) tall and staple horticultural fleece to the sides. Adult carrot flies are low flying, rarely getting more than 45cm (18in) above soil level, so this barrier keeps them off the developing crop and prevents them laying their eggs there. The result? No eggs, no maggots and no tunnelling.

It's also a good idea to sow carrot seeds sparingly to avoid having to thin out the resulting seedlings. This is because the adult carrot flies have a keen sense of smell and are attracted to the odour of the foliage when it is crushed as the seedlings are pulled up.

TIP
Planting other strongly scented crops such as onions or garlic can help deter carrot flies from their prize.

Enjoy the sweetest corn

Time to plant: May/June

Freshly picked sweetcorn is a real treat in late summer, but however much you love it, try to restrain yourself and grow only one variety. Having more than one risks cross-pollination, which results in a less sweet crop.

The breeders have been busy when it comes to sweetcorn and you'll find a great selection of different varieties in seed catalogues. Look for ones that have been bred to produce reliable results in our less than reliable climate, such as 'Conqueror'.

When planting, arrange plants in a block instead of rows. This will help to increase the rate of successful pollination for this wind-pollinated crop, even if you only have a few plants.

As soon as the golden tassels are starting to turn brown, the cobs are ready to harvest. Leave them on too long and the kernels will become tougher and starchier. Cook the cobs immediately after harvesting, because the moment they leave the plant the sugars in the kernels start converting into starches.

TIP
If you can't resist growing more than one variety of sweetcorn, make sure you pick 'tendersweet' ones, such as 'Lark', as these don't need to be isolated from other varieties.

Keep leeks healthy

Time to sow: March–April

The key to keeping leeks healthy starts from the first sowings. While in most areas you can sow leeks outdoors in March or April, it's best to sow them in pots or trays at this time, as this seems to dramatically reduce the number of casualties due to pests and diseases in those first weeks.

Sow leek seeds thinly so that the tiny grass-like seedlings can later be transplanted into fresh compost in a larger pot, where they will rapidly increase in size. By early summer they should be ready for planting out in the garden.

Leeks are not a particularly fussy crop and will do well in most soils, especially well-manured, heavy ones. The only problem you are likely to encounter is fungal rust, to which they are very prone – this is visible as orange or brown marks that cover the leaves and stems.

Rust-resistant, or at least tolerant, varieties are the best leeks to grow, as there is no chemical control available to gardeners. Good ones to try include 'Neptune', 'Autumn Mammoth 2' and 'Alvito'. However, don't be surprised if some rust does appear, especially if late summer and early autumn is rather wet.

TIP
Never put infected plants on the compost heap. If you do, the problem will carry over to the next year, because the fungal spores will remain in the compost.

Successful parsnips
Time to sow: spring

Although it is worth growing a few parsnips from seed, it has to be said that they are not the easiest crop and can be very slow to germinate. To get good-shaped roots you need to take extra care with soil preparation and maintenance.

Good parsnips start from the ground up, which means creating a deep, fairly fine-textured soil that is free from stones. For the best results, the soil should, ideally, be neutral to alkaline.

As germination is both slow and somewhat erratic in parsnips, sow the seeds in groups, or stations, placing each clutch of three or four at regular intervals along the row. Space each group of seeds 10–15cm (4–6in) apart, and make each row 30cm (1ft) from the next.

Good weed control is essential, especially as the plants take a while to appear. Keep the row well marked to avoid hoeing off the first leaves when they do finally come through. By sowing a few seeds where one plant is required, you can afford to lose some. Thin out the less vigorous plants later on.

TIP
If your soil is not perfect you can still grow parsnips, but choose shorter-rooted varieties such as 'Avonresister', which also has resistance to canker.

Warm up your soil   Time to do: early spring

Many crops fail completely if the soil is too wet and cold when the seeds are sown early in the season, so it's often worth waiting a week or two for conditions to improve. However, if you are impatient or simply want to bring on a few crops early, it's a good idea to warm the soil before sowing.

Polythene mini-polytunnels or a row of cloches will warm soil admirably while also keeping off excess rain. Try to get this sort of protection in place a few weeks before planting, but even a couple of days will make a difference.

This is not a process requiring precise assessment of temperatures, it's simply a case of taking the spring chill off the soil to provide better conditions for germination and seedling growth.

If you're trying to encourage early development of seedlings and young plants, cloches or mini-polytunnels tend to work best. As the plants grow, these can be replaced with fleece tunnels, before the plants are finally exposed to the outside world.

TIP
On dry soils, a couple of layers of horticultural fleece will help warm up the soil while still allowing moisture through.

Grow better spuds Time to do: spring

Potatoes are pretty easy plants to grow, but they do fall victim to a few problems that can be reduced by spending a little time using the technique of 'earthing up'.

Earthing up spuds – basically covering the new shoots with a layer of turned earth to create a long mound – is essential when the young shoots are around 15–20cm (6–8in) high in spring. The main reason for doing this is to prevent frost damage, but it also reduces the chances of harvesting tubers with a green tinge – which are poisonous to eat. Some varieties grow tubers close to the surface, and regular earthing up reduces greening.

Tubers buried a little deeper also seem to be less likely to be infected quickly if potato blight strikes. This devastating disease often attacks in periods of warm, wet weather and can cause the whole crop to rot. The spores that cause the disease wash down into the soil from infected plants, so the extra soil between the tuber and the soil surface can help to prevent the crop getting ruined.

When the potato shoots have reached about 25cm (10in), use a rake or spade to flick the soil upward. Work your way along the row of potatoes, carefully covering the shoots to create a neat mound. Just a few weeks later, plenty of foliage will sprout up as the shoots push through the mound.

TIP
Earthing up is a little extra work, but it pays off at harvest time when the crop is easier to lift and produces fewer damaged tubers.

Easy onions   Time to plant: March/April

While onions can be raised from seed, it's much easier to grow them from little bulbs called 'sets', which can be bought from garden centres or are available via mail order.

Before planting sets, dig the soil over thoroughly, removing any weeds and large stones.

Onions look best in army-straight rows, so this is the time to get out your gardening line. If you do not own one already you could improvise by just tying a length of twine or string to two pieces of quite sturdy cane.

Simply ease each small onion into the soil so that the tips are left protruding. If you want large onions, space the sets about 10cm (4in) apart. But if you prefer smaller ones, space them about 6cm (2½in) apart.

For the next few weeks, cover the newly planted rows with netting. If the sets are left uncovered they are likely to be removed by inquisitive birds, whereas if they are covered until they have rooted, you should be able to keep them all in place.

TIP
The main crop is usually planted in early to mid-spring, but you could try putting in a few in mid-autumn the following year for an early spring crop.

Keep cropping for longer

Late summer is the time of year when so many of the plants you have grown and nurtured are filling your plate, and maybe your freezer too. However, although your trug may be full, this is not a time to rest on your laurels. There are several simple ways to keep fruit and vegetables cropping for as long as possible.

If the weather is dry, regular watering will help to prolong crops, but in late summer it is even more important to avoid wetting the plants' foliage, as diseases such as mildew and rust thrive in damp conditions.

Plants such as tomatoes, aubergines and peppers will carry on producing useful harvests if given a bit of protection from cooler temperatures.

To keep temperatures around plants a little higher, use horticultural fleece held in place with ground pegs or bricks, or mini fleece tunnels. Alternatively, old net curtains work just as well – they are both strong and economical. For individual plants, sturdy clear plastic bell cloches are a great solution.

TIP
Whenever possible, pick crops and eat them straight away. Harvesting little and often means everything is in peak condition and packed full of flavour, juice and vitamins.

Try mangetout peas

Time to sow: spring–early summer

The word mangetout translates literally as 'eat all', and that is precisely what you can do with this delicious pea. Forget fiddly shelling – with mangetouts you can eat the tender pod as well as the developing peas within, so they are well worth a spot in your veg garden.

Mangetouts thrive in a sunny spot on a neutral to alkaline soil – preferably one that has had plenty of organic matter incorporated during the previous winter.

Seed catalogues contain mouth-watering descriptions of mangetout varieties. Favourites are 'Oregon Sugar Pod', 'Delikata' and 'Sugar Snap'. The latter two are suitable for eating as mangetouts, or you can leave the pods on the plants to develop fully, then shell them like normal peas.

Sow the seed from early spring until early summer. Remember to harvest crops regularly, because edible peas, much like their ornamental relative the sweet pea, will soon slow down and cease to crop prolifically if they are not promptly picked.

Harvest when the pods are 7.5cm (3in) or less in length and they will melt in your mouth.

TIP
Mangetouts are delicious lightly cooked and simply drenched in butter or tossed in a salad or stir-fry. If eaten shortly after harvesting, they beat any other peas you can ever buy in the shops.

Fuss-free leeks

Time to sow: spring

A lot of people seem to shy away from growing leeks, perhaps because they are too closely associated with horticultural shows rather than good eating. Yet this really is an easy crop and a great way to provide delicious vegetables at a less productive time of year.

The traditional technique of 'earthing up' leeks can put people off – but it's actually very easy. All you do is plant the leeks quite shallowly, about 7.5cm (3in), in a pencil-thick hole which you fill up with water, not earth. Then, three or more times during the growing season you simply draw up the soil around the stems, about 5cm (2in) each time.

By early to mid-autumn, the first leeks are ready for lifting. Loosen the soil beneath the plant with a fork, then they are easily harvested by hand. Soil still clinging to the base can be shaken back on to the bed or added to the compost bin, together with the outer leaves.

Mid- to late-cropping varieties are particularly hardy, and some can safely be left in the soil throughout winter.

TIP
Earthing up produces well-blanched stems, but it is quite time-consuming. To avoid the bother, simply plant them deeper, to about 15–20cm (6–8in). This makes leeks a truly easy, trouble-free crop.

Brassicas under attack
Time to do: spring–summmer

Pest attacks on brassicas can leave your cabbages, cauliflowers, Brussels sprouts and broccoli looking like rather sad specimens and can drastically reduce your eventual harvest. But there are simple ways in which you can reduce the risk of attack by certain pests.

Keep pests at bay by covering crops with fleece or fine-mesh netting. Support it with a series of wire hoops to create a tunnel over the plants. This allows them space to grow and prevents the covering from touching the leaves – thereby inadvertently allowing the pests a way in.

If plants are protected from the moment they are planted out, you can avoid the caterpillars of cabbage white butterflies. By covering them, you will not need to spray the pests and you can look forward to top-quality veg for your dinner plate.

Pigeons are also a real pain when it comes to brassicas, as they love to eat the young shoots and will shred plants to pieces, but they can also be discouraged by netting.

TIP
Don't chuck out old CDs or used bits of tin foil, instead hang these and anything that sparkles and glints in the light above crops to scare off greedy birds.

Success with beans
Time to sow: spring

The taste and texture of home-grown beans is second to none, especially climbing French beans. These are similar in taste to runner beans but seem to produce more reliable crops and have fewer problems with bees cutting their way into the back of the flowers.

Raise beans in trays or pots under glass as this produces better results than sowing outdoors, minimises the risk of seeds failing to germinate when the weather suddenly turns very wet and cold, and also cuts down on slug damage.

Watch out for frosts – If one is forecast, protect plants with a cloche. Similarly, if a spell of very dry weather arrives, make sure the plants are kept well watered, especially those that have recently been planted out.

Climbing beans need support, and a wigwam of wooden poles or bamboo canes is a popular choice. Firmly tie four or five canes together with twine or raffia and drive them into the soil really well. Even on a heavy soil, which is relatively supportive, the canes need to go in at a depth of 13–15cm (5–6in). A sudden strong gust of wind can cause an inadequately secured support to topple, especially once it is carrying a heavy crop of foliage and beans.

TIP
Steam or microwave purple or golden varieties to keep their colour after cooking.

Move your crops around

Sowing one type of crop into the same patch of soil again and again will cause a build-up of pests and diseases. Having attracted the pest or disease in one year, by replanting the same crop you are providing it again with host plants on which it will thrive. Instead, you need to change the crop, so the pests and diseases die out. This is known as crop rotation.

Many problems with crops can be avoided if you move different vegetables from one place to another each year. Different types of crop require varying amounts of nutrients.

By swapping the main groups of vegetables around in a regular order, you can make the most efficient use of the nutrients in the soil. Anyone wanting to grow veg using minimal fertiliser should use this system.

Crops also utilise different trace elements in the soil. If you grow the same thing year after year, your soil will gradually become impoverished in certain trace elements. Herbs are very sensitive to this and appear to lose flavour in tired soil, especially tarragon and mint.

TIP
If you have four veg beds, reserve one for roots, one for legumes, one for brassicas and one for potatoes.

Companion planting

The principle of companion planting is to grow one plant next to another to protect a crop from pests and diseases, or to help with pollination and hence increase your harvest.

In many cases the fragrance of the companion plant, nasty or nice, will either repel the pest or mask the scent of the vulnerable crop you're trying to protect. In the second instance, the pest doesn't realise you have tasty food in your garden and goes off to look elsewhere.

Surrounding tomatoes, chillies, aubergines and peppers with tagetes (French marigolds) is a classic example of companion planting. The smell of the foliage is repellent to whitefly, and thus keeps it away from your edible crops.

Like tagetes, basil also protects many different crops. Whitefly love basil above almost anything else, making it the perfect companion plant for tomatoes and aubergines, which tend to suffer with the same infestation. They'll go for your pots of basil in preference to your tomatoes!

Another popular way to deter one of the scourges of the veg garden, carrot fly, is to interplant onions, garlic or leeks with your carrots. It is thought the oniony smell masks that of the carrots, which confuses the pest.

TIP
Nasturtiums have several uses: their strong smell keeps aphids off broccoli and squash plants, and caterpillars love them, so plant them with cabbages to act as a decoy.

Colourful carrots   Time to sow: early spring–midsummer

Growing your own carrots can be a real eye-opener. You'll be amazed at the fantastically sweet, strong flavour of some varieties. What's more, they're now available in a startling array of colours (although sometimes at the expense of flavour and texture).

Choose your carrot variety carefully and you'll get that satisfying feeling of pulling your own carrots and, just minutes later, finding out what a carrot should really taste like.

'Purple Dragon' is one of the best of the colourful varieties. To say it is extraordinary to look at would be an understatement. With its really strong, dark purple skin, it's such a surprise to find the tempting orange flesh within. The texture and flavour makes it an absolute pleasure to eat raw, steamed or in a stir-fry.

'Kinbi' is one of the best of the paler colours. It has an extremely pretty yellow root – much brighter yellow than most – that would add interest to any salad. It has a slightly stumpy shape and a better flavour than other varieties without orange flesh.

TIP
If you can, try before you buy and don't fall for a carrot because of its unusual colour – there is a white variety called 'Belgian White', but it is rather lacking in flavour.

Try something different
Time to sow: April/May

If you're a fan of broccoli, then you should try some of the tasty purple-sprouting varieties for a really tender, tasty vegetable in winter and spring.

Sow broccoli seeds in April or May into a seedbed of well-dug and well-raked soil.

Keep the area clear of weeds and thin the seedlings to about 8cm (3in) apart for sturdy plants. It is important to keep the weeds down, as they will compete with your crop and large weeds will shade the seedlings, making them weaker, more spindly and more prone to disease.

When the seedlings are about 8cm (3in) tall with five or six leaves, they can be transferred from the seedbed to their final positions. Check the seed packet of the variety you choose, but it is usually best to leave about 60cm (2ft) between the plants.

There are plenty of excellent varieties available, including 'Rudolph', which produces rich purple spears from around Christmas time. Another good one to try is 'Claret', which is an F1 hybrid with wine-red spears that crops heavily from about April for a month or so.

TIP
Always keep a few seeds spare in case there are any disasters with the seedlings, such as an early slug attack or a trampling child.

Keeping warm in winter

Wrap up your soil in winter and you'll be rewarded in spring with warmer, more workable ground.

Carpet and black plastic are both excellent ways to cover bare ground during winter. First, they stop any weeds growing, and it's staggering how many will grow, even in the depths of winter. Second, they keep the soil warm and workable, allowing you to simply lift them off an area and dig it over in frosty weather when others can't touch their plot. It's best to avoid working the soil when frozen, as you destroy its structure.

Cast-off hessian-backed stair carpets are perfect as they can be laid in lengths, unlike a huge square piece from a room. Foam-backed, nylon carpets are awful, as they disintegrate, leaving bits all over your vegetable plot.

Alternatively, use flattened cardboard boxes weighted down with stones and bricks, or black plastic sheeting with slits to allow rain through. It has to be black to absorb warmth from the sun. But it's better to invest in some woven ground-cover material from the garden centre, because it's porous and lasts for ages. Buy it off the roll rather than pre-packed, as it tends to be cheaper that way.

Feeding know-how

Time to act: autumn, winter and summer

Confused about what, when and how to feed your veg? Don't worry – it's not as difficult as it seems, and there are several easy methods that will stop your plants going hungry.

You'll go a long way to maintaining the fertility and structure of your soil by simply covering the ground with an 8–10cm (3–4in) deep layer of organic matter, such as well-rotted manure, each year. Spread it on the soil in autumn and the worms will work it into the ground over the winter. This is particularly beneficial on light soils where heavy winter rainfall can cause nutrients to be washed out. Any organic matter remaining on the surface in spring can then be simply forked in.

Manure is as much as most plants require, as over-feeding can produce soft, floppy growth. Pelleted chicken manure is useful as a fertiliser, but check it is from an organic source if your plot is organic. The pellets can be incorporated with a good degree of accuracy and have a noticeable effect on the plants. Spring is the best time to apply it to most crops.

Fruiting plants benefit from feeding with a fertiliser that is high in potash, such as tomato food.

TIP
Where quick results are required, fertiliser will be taken up faster by the plants if it is applied as a liquid feed to the roots, or sprayed on the leaves.

Enjoy a late crop of peas   Time to sow: July

Freshly picked, home-grown peas are so irresistible that it's hard to get them into the kitchen without munching them as you harvest them. With this in mind, it's worth sowing a few late plants in July to give you a fresh burst of cropping right into autumn.

By autumn, pea plants sown earlier in the year will have long since finished producing anything useful, and will quite often have succumbed to an attack of mildew too.

Sowing peas direct into the soil as late as July usually works better than earlier sowings. If it is a bad year for slugs, though, you may prefer to raise the plants in cells or modules. Plant them out while they are still small because these young plants always have a really good root system. Provided the compost is just slightly moist when you remove them from the cell, the roots hold together well and are unlikely to get damaged.

Using a trowel, dig a small hole for each plant then pop them all in and water the whole area thoroughly. Drive supports into the soil close to the plants as soon as they are transplanted in order to minimise disturbance. The plantlets soon start to cling on with their tendrils.

TIP
Twiggy sticks make the most attractive supports for peas. You can buy them from garden centres or you can save some suitable, well-branched prunings of your own.

Get composting

A compost bin – or preferably two or three – is something most gardeners want, and indeed need. It's amazing how much compostable material even a small garden can produce.

Autumn clearing always produces compostable waste; everything from old potato plants and brassica foliage, to the odd courgette and bean plant that is past its useful life. Almost any vegetable waste can be composted. Avoid meat and cooked foods, however, as these can attract vermin, and never use perennial weeds such as dandelions or diseased material, as these may not be killed by the composting process.

Whether you have a large or small bin, the contents must be turned to aerate them and make sure everything is mixed in so that all parts are subjected to the higher temperatures at the centre.

Once the compost has rotted down, it can be dug into the soil to improve its structure or used as a mulch on the surface to hold moisture in the soil below.

You can make one from old pallets or floorboards, or many local councils sell plastic bins at discount prices.

TIP
Don't bin kitchen peelings, put them in a worm bin where they can be converted into compost and liquid feed (right).

Make a wigwam

Good, robust wigwams are a brilliant addition to any vegetable patch and are perfect for supporting a range of climbing crops, including beans and pumpkins.

To ensure that the structure doesn't blow away, you need the verticals of your wigwam to sink a good 15–20cm (6–8in) into the ground. It should then stand at least 1.8m (6ft), or even better 2.1m (7ft), up in the air. Once any bean, sweet pea or nasturtium is growing at full tilt it will swamp anything smaller.

You can buy big wigwams from a good willow supplier, or you can make your own. You will need at least eight straight sticks, such as hazel or silver birch, or bamboo canes, along with tarred string, Flexi-ties or coated wire.

Draw a circle about 1m (3ft) in diameter in the soil with a stick. Poke one of your uprights in, then another about 30cm (1ft) away, then the next, and so on. You'll then have a circle of wooden uprights. Gather them up at the top and tie them together with string, Flexi-tie or coated wire.

TIP
Make sure the wigwam is tall enough for your purposes – to make them easy to put on the roof of a car, most frames available at garden centres are far too small.

Beat blight

It might not be obvious at first glance, but tomatoes and potatoes are close cousins. Sadly, this also means that they both suffer from the devastating disease called blight.

Plants with blight will suddenly look like they have been frosted or suffered a severe blast of windburn, then the next day they look charred and that's it – the whole lot have to be ripped out and disposed of.

Tomato and potato plants affected by blight have to be treated with a fortnightly spray of fungicide to ensure the plants survive. This fungus easily transfers between the two crops and tends to hang around. Without the fungicide your whole carefully tended crop may well collapse in two or three days in August or early September, when the weather is wet and mild.

If you prefer to avoid the use of chemicals, grow tomato plants inside where they're more protected. Earthing up potato plants also helps to protect the tubers. Remove any diseased growth as soon as you see it and never compost it.

TIP
Some varieties have been bred to resist blight, such as tomato 'Ferline' and potato 'Sarpo Mira'.

Veg in the flower beds Time to plant: spring

You don't need a huge garden to grow your own veg – they grow equally well mixed in with the flowers in a border as they do in their own separate space.

The border in the picture looks as delicious as it tastes and is just 90cm x 1.8m (3ft x 6ft). A bed like this, harvested regularly when the crops are small and tasty, allows you to space plants more closely than generally recommended, so you can squeeze a surprising amount in. This bed produced a copious supply of salad veg, including lettuce, beetroot and mini-sweetcorn, all summer. It didn't cost the earth either, as most of the crops can be grown from seed.

For the best results, plant your edible border in the sunniest spot you can find in the garden and prepare the ground carefully. This will help to ensure good growth and encourage your crops to ripen well.

Keep the border well watered, especially in its early stages and during any prolonged dry spells, and particularly if your soil is stony and free-draining.

Watch out for garden pests such as greenfly, caterpillars and slugs, and deal with them swiftly before they make inroads into your crop.

TIP
A border like this should fill out within eight weeks of planting. Of course, some crops mature faster than others, but by sowing a pinch of seed every few weeks you can replace those already harvested.

Get an allotment

If you're frustrated by the lack of space in your own garden, or don't want to grow veg among your flowers, why not get your hands on some new ground by renting an allotment?

Your local council will tell you where the nearest allotments to you are. Prices vary considerably, but the rent shouldn't break the bank – they tend to start from around £6 a year, although in London you could pay up to £60.

Many councils include free clearing and rotavating of the plot in the price to help you get started, so it's worth asking.

When it comes to choosing your plot, it pays to find out if there is a site representative. They will be able to tell you where the best soil is, point out any frost pockets, and outline which areas are windswept. Steer clear of steep slopes unless you're prepared to terrace the site, and look out for a plot near a water tap – it will save you leg-work in summer.

If you can, pick a plot close to well-tended areas. The last thing you want is someone else's weed seeds blowing into your plot, or roots creeping under the fence.

Most allotment rental periods run from autumn to autumn, so in areas of high demand, be sure to get your name on the waiting list by summer.

TIP
For help with plots or tips on allotments, join the National Society for Allotment and Leisure Gardeners.

Make raised beds

Time to do: any time

Raised beds not only make a vegetable garden look neat and tidy but they offer a number of practical benefits too.

Raised beds are a real saving grace if your garden soil is poor, as they can be filled with imported topsoil or loam-based compost to provide better growing conditions. If you build the raised beds around 1.2m (4ft) wide, you can tend them from the sides and never need to walk on them, so you won't get problems with soil compaction. Leave 45cm (18in) between beds to allow wheelbarrow access.

Organic matter can easily be added by simply covering the soil with a thick layer of compost or well-rotted manure in autumn and letting the worms pull it into the soil over the winter.

The raised height of the beds also means that drainage is good – a relief when your garden soil is clay and often soggy. Gardeners with back problems will also appreciate the raised height as it cuts down on the amount of bending needed to reach the crops.

Beds are simple to make or you can buy ready-made modular systems. To keep costs down, you can always make them using recycled old timber, such as scaffolding boards.

TIP
If you can, run the beds from north to south to give your crops even sunlight levels.

Plant asparagus

Time to plant: March

Asparagus is a real gourmet treat, and home-grown spears are far superior to those in the shops. They're quite easy to grow and well worth the effort for their flavour.

Good varieties of asparagus include: 'Connover's Colossal', which has a superb flavour, and 'Backlim' and 'Franklim' which produce consistently high yields.

Plant one-year-old crowns in March, 45cm (18in) apart, into ground that is rich, well-drained and well-manured, and cover the crowns with several inches of soil. Don't cut the spears, let them grow into mature plants and when these turn dead and brown at the end of the autumn, cut the ferny leaves off at ground level and build up the soil around the crowns. The following year manure the bed well, but don't cut the spears. In the third year, crop the spears lightly for about four weeks, then from the fourth year onwards, crop from the end of April until the middle of summer. Leave all buds that appear after this date to grow into ferns.

Asparagus plants make a slow start but the same crowns will then crop successfully for more than 20 years.

Although slugs can be tiresome, the only real pests are asparagus beetles. These cream, red and black pests have to be despatched by hand.

TIP

Cook asparagus the day it's picked. Break off the tough ends and steam slender spears. With thicker spears, loosely tie them together and place upright in a deep pan of water so the stems boil and the tips steam above the water. Cover and cook for 5–10 minutes, depending on their thickness.

Index

Picture credits

BBC Books and *Gardeners' World Magazine* would like to thank the following for providing photographs. While every effort has been made to trace and acknowledge all photographers, we would like to apologize should there be any errors or omissions.

Mark Bolton p11, p13; Paul Debois p95; Stephen Hamilton p4, p17, p33, p41, p43,p45, p53, p67, p81, p99, p107, p139, p149, p169, p171, p173, p177, p179, p193, p201, p209; Mike Harding p105; Sarah Heneghan p37, p39, p45, p89, p91, p93, p109, p125, p127, p131, p133, p137, p153, p157, p163, p165, p167, p189, p195; Anne Hyde p35; Jason Ingram p25, p27, p29, p31, p61, p87, p95, p97, p115, p121; Lynn Keddie p5, p101, p103, p119; Stephen Marwood p143; Ben Murphy p21, p23; Noel Murphy p5, p6, 181, p187; Tim Sandall p5, p9, p57, p59, p63, p71, p73, p75, p83, p85, p117, p129, p135, p141, p145, p147, p151, p175, p185, p197, p199; Freia Turland/Dig Pictures p4, p15, p19, p203; William Shaw p65, p69, p77, p155, p161; Nick Smith p159, p191, p205; Simon Wheeler p79; Jo Whitworth p113

With thanks to Lisa Buckland, Lizzy Gayton, Pippa Greenwood, Jekka McVicar, Jane Moore and Bob Purnell.

Also available from BBC *Gardeners' World* magazine and BBC Books: